T0355506

Securing the Sacred
Religion, National Security, and the Western State

Robert Bosco offers a detailed, comparative analysis of the ways in which the United Kingdom, France, and the United States attempt to engage with religion for reasons of national security. In the wake of 9/11, political elites in these three states converged on a common understanding which framed the problem of Islam not as the traditional "clash of civilizations" but rather as a clash within Islam itself in which Western secular democracies must take sides. Using detailed case studies, Bosco demonstrates the implementation and varied success of this strategy in three different contexts—at home in Britain and France, and abroad, in the case of the United States. *Securing the Sacred* enriches the study of religion and international politics by framing religion as a national security conundrum and calling attention to the interest which contemporary secular political powers have vested in the development and reform of religions.

Robert M. Bosco is Assistant Professor of International Studies at Centre College.

CONFIGURATIONS: CRITICAL STUDIES OF WORLD POLITICS

Patrick Thaddeus Jackson, series editor

Titles in the series:

Securing the Sacred

Religion, National Security, *and the* Western State

Robert M. Bosco

University of Michigan Press
Ann Arbor

First paperback edition 2016
Copyright © by the University of Michigan 2014
All rights reserved

Published in the United States of America by the
University of Michigan Press
Printed and bound by CPI Group (UK) Ltd, Croydon, CR0 4YY

2019   2018   2017   2016   5   4   3   2

A CIP catalog record for this book is available from the British Library.

Library of Congress Cataloging-in-Publication Data

Bosco, Robert M.
    Securing the sacred : religion, national security, and the western state / Robert M. Bosco.
        pages   cm — (Configurations : critical studies of world politics)
        Includes bibliographical references and index.
        ISBN 978-0-472-11922-6 (cloth : alk. paper) — ISBN 978-0-472-12009-3 (e-book)
        1. Religion and politics.   2. National security—Religious aspects.
    3. Secularization.   4. Church and state.   I. Title.

    BL65.P7B659   2014
    322'.1091821—dc23

                                                            2013036756

ISBN 978-0-472-03675-2 (pbk. : alk. paper)

Contents

Acknowledgments

I owe many debts of gratitude to those who helped to make this book a reality. This book owes its origin to my longstanding interest—students and friends would say obsession—with the study of religion in international affairs. My journey into this topic began under the tutelage of Mustapha Kamal Pasha, then at American University's School of International Service. The advice, encouragement, and friendship he provided set me on a voyage of rich intellectual reward. A summer at Boston University's Institute for Culture, Religion & World Affairs put more wind in my sails, and Dr. Jennifer Sterling-Folker at the University of Connecticut urged me to follow the topic wherever it may lead. A year's fellowship in Religion in International Affairs at Harvard University's Belfer Center challenged me to clarify and defend.

At the University of Michigan Press, I would like to thank Patrick Thaddeus Jackson for encouraging me with the enticing proposition that I have, here, a book. Editor Melody Herr gave my project a warm reception from the very beginning and inspired me with her contagious enthusiasm. No first-time author could have asked for a more energetic and supportive team.

I also thank the faculty, students, and administration of Centre College. The college's generous faculty development grants helped fund the travels and translations that made this book possible. I want to say a special thank you to Brittany Faye Tucker for her help with translations from the French. I would not have been able to complete the French case without her assistance.

Finally, I would like to thank my family, especially my wife, colleague, and best friend, Dina. Throughout she has been a source of love, support, help, and humor. I dedicate this book to her.

Foreword

The idea of the *Configurations* book series is to combine cutting-edge conceptual and theoretical work with detailed case studies so as to demonstrate, in concrete ways, what novel insights such combinations can generate. Robert Bosco's book is that rare combination of a timely work on a subject in the popular consciousness that also stands as analytically and theoretically insightful and innovative. This is a rare feat indeed and I am pleased to say that Bosco pulls it off elegantly.

The key point of departure for Bosco is securitization theory, which maintains that we need to account for the ways in which various objects and phenomena in world politics are made to seem threatening instead of merely assuming that they *are* (or are not) threatening. From this beginning, securitization theorists have produced a variety of engaging works about how poverty, environmental change, immigration, and the like have been politically portrayed as requiring a security-based state response; these works have also helped to broaden the theoretical definition of "security" to more closely mirror the way that the term is used in contemporary social and political discussions. But securitization theory traditionally suffers from a key omission, which is that it rarely if ever provides a compelling answer to the more general question of why some attempts to "securitize" an object (say, terrorism) succeed while other attempts to "securitize" an object (say, education) are not as successful: despite frequent efforts by political elites, gaps in test scores between countries are not as readily understood as a "security threat" as indiscriminate violence against civilians is. And there are practical consequences: we have in the United States a Department of Homeland Security, but national educational policy is a crazy-quilt of local regulations and standards. It *matters* that some things are successfully securitized while others are not.

In this respect, Bosco's disclosure of a pattern in the securitization of religion across his three case studies represents an important conclusion: states that tried to securitize domestically were less successful than states that tried to securitize internationally. The French and British attempts to promote "moderate Islam" on security grounds within their countries were considerably less efficacious than the U.S. efforts to promote "moderate Islam" abroad, and this in turn has to do with the way that the state has been constituted as secular and liberal. The deeper history of the secular state tradition thus places important boundaries on the kinds of things that can be successfully securitized domestically, while the deeper history of the international as a realm of danger opens possibilities even for a secular state to successfully get involved in religious issues. Methodologically speaking, Bosco's work unveils the specific combination of factors in sequence that produce the different observed outcomes; instead of single causal factors, we have causal mechanisms assembled in complex configurations. Theoretically speaking, Bosco's work helps to concretize the different possibilities afforded by state traditions in contemporary world politics. And practically speaking, Bosco's work forces us to think again about the "threatening" nature of religion, and pause to unpack the processes that go into the production of religion as a threat—either a threat to the state from outside its borders, or a threat to the boundaries between the state and civil society in Europe and the United States.

This is a book I am very pleased to be able to offer as part of the *Configurations* book series.

PATRICK THADDEUS JACKSON
Series Editor, Configurations
Professor of International Relations and Associate Dean for
Undergraduate Education in the School of International
Service at the American University, Washington, D.C.

Introduction

Religion as a National Security Enigma

After 9/11, religion reappeared as a national security enigma in the West. For many, the events of that day had an irreducibly religious dimension. For reasons of national security, the sacred could no longer be ignored. On the other hand, it remained unclear exactly how to engage with religious ideas and actors without undermining the legitimacy of the secular state, creating new *in*securities for all. This is the paradox, I argue, that states face regarding religion and national security in a post–9/11 world.

This book is about how three secular states—Britain, France, and the U.S.—perceive the relationship between religion and national security and grapple with it in their own ways, both at home and abroad. Official national security strategies, presidential and prime ministerial speeches, internal documents, and confidential meetings provide a wealth of evidence that after 9/11 all three governments engaged in wide-ranging efforts to encourage religious reform, especially within Islam. Similar efforts, however, led to different outcomes—some successful, others not. What can account for these similarities and differences, and what can scholars of religion and International Relations learn from these cases?

I find that when secular states engage with religious actors for purposes of national security at the domestic level of analysis, religious communities are often alienated because questions of social and political loyalty become bound up with "correct" interpretations of their religion. The secular state cannot avoid here the appearance of manipulating religious belief for its own national security ends, thus straining its legitimacy. Abroad, it is easier to separate matters of political loyalty from the promotion of certain interpretations of religion over others; as with the case of the U.S., encouraging the development of certain interpretations of Islam can be outsourced to reliable state allies who can back up their programs of religious restructuring with coercive force. In the final analysis, religion is easier securitized at the international, rather than the domestic, level of analysis. In any case, however, secular states frame religion as a matter of national security at their peril.

RELIGION IN GLOBAL POLITICS: THE WIDER CONTEXT

For most of its existence, the modern study of global politics proceeded under the assumption that international politics is *high politics:* the realm in which great powers, measured by material capability, compete with each other for security and survival. Religious beliefs may impact the personal predilections of policymakers, exacerbate a distant communal conflict, or retard the progression of a "Third World" society toward socialist or capitalist modernity. By and large, however, religious actors and beliefs did not and should not have a significant role to play in international politics. For religion had been banished from interstate relations since the age of Westphalia: religion as a reason for war, conquest, or intervention in the affairs of others was the preserve of an early modern Europe struggling to emerge into our more enlightened times. Modern states have since come into being, and the most powerful of these have escaped religion's volatility and fashioned a world less savage. Reinforced intellectually by sociological theories of secularization that underpinned Western social science for the greater part of the 20th century, this "Westphalian" narrative solidified as common sense in the scholarship and practice of international politics (Philpott 2002; Carlson and Owens 2003; Thomas 2005).

It was not until the end of the Cold War, and slowly even then, that scholars began to turn their attention to the role that religion plays in international affairs. By the early 1990s a number of scholars began to perceive that collective obsession with Cold War politics had allowed religion to remain hidden from view. If one looked closely, however, one could detect that a "longing for an indigenous form of religious politics free from the taint of Western culture"—that is, free from *both* communism and Western free-market capitalism—had been brewing around the world all throughout the 1980s and 1990s (Juergensmeyer 1993, 1). A new generation of activists in Egypt, India, Sri Lanka and elsewhere, disenchanted with the promises and premises of competing Western ideologies, instead sought a new ethnic and religious nationalism that "view(ed) religion as a hopeful alternative, a base for criticism and change" (2). To be sure, the rise of religious alternatives to Western intellectual constructions was not unique to these decades. In his famous 1968 study of Islam in Indonesia and Morocco, for example, Clifford Geertz argued that as the "secularization of thought" (by which he meant Anglo-European conceptions of modern science and economics) proceeds, a counterreaction will take form and coalesce as religious nationalism (Geertz 1968, 104 +ff.). What did seem new, however, was the sheer scale on which religion was reentering the public realm. Looking back over the 1980s at the end of the Cold War one scholar observed that "religious traditions throughout the world are refusing to accept the marginal and privatized role which theories of modernity as well as theories of secularization had reserved for them" (Casanova 1994). Faced with mounting evidence, even secularism's staunchest defenders began to speak instead of a "*de*secularization of the world" (Berger 1999; emphasis mine).

This "desecularization of the world" surely had implications for national and international security, but the precise role that revived religious energies would play in the international realm remained a matter of conjecture. Samuel Huntington famously essayed that the clashes of the future will be between and among civilizations, with civilizations defined in large part by their religious values and beliefs (Huntington 1993). Others argued on hard empirical evidence that "a growing gap has opened up between the value systems of rich and poor countries, making religious differences *increasingly* salient" (Norris and Inglehart 2004, 217). The same authors concluded, however, in contrast to Huntington, that "there is no reason why this growing cultural divergence must inevitably lead to violent conflict, but it is a cleavage that fanatics and demagogues can seize, to use for their own ends" (217). Religion's return seemed a double-edged sword for international security: religion appeared as an "ambivalent" phenomenon that could contribute both to increased intolerance and violence, and to the peaceful resolution of conflict (Appleby 2000; see also Rudolph and Piscatori 1997).

Religion's increasing role in international politics was an especially pressing issue from the perspective of policymakers in the state, particularly Western states that understood themselves to have long settled the question of the relationship between religion and the public sphere, albeit with different varieties of secularism (Hurd 2008). Whether *laiciste,* or owing its roots to the Judeo-Christian tradition, secularism remained a discourse of power, a "strategy to manage the relationship between religion and politics" (5).[1]

After the end of the Cold War, however, it seemed that this relationship, often taken to be settled, needed to be rethought. Reinvigorated, public religion worldwide struck at the very foundations of the liberal conception of security: legitimacy and political obligation. Around the world, religious activists questioned "the rationale for having a state, the moral basis for politics, and the reasons why a state should elicit loyalty" (Juergensmeyer 1993, 7). Secular states would now have to think again about religion and, for purposes of national security, engage with religious ideas and actors in the public sphere without threatening the boundaries between secular and sacred that gave these states their core identities. As one scholar put it "the public-private distinction . . . must be recast" in the light of new "ad hoc alliances" between states and non-state religious actors (Appleby 2000, 301–2). Indeed, since the end of the Cold War, *failure* to engage with religious ideas and actors—not the *presence* of religion on the international scene—appeared as a new national security liability. After 9/11, Western, secular states faced this problem more acutely than ever before.

METHOD, THEORY, AND ARGUMENT

In this book I analyze the contemporary relationship between religion and national security in the West by first separating state discourse from policy, and then looking at the interaction between the two at different levels of analysis. By discourse, I refer to how the problem of religion and national security is framed in spoken or written language. As I show throughout this book, post–9/11 Western state discourse about religion attempted to short-circuit the concept of a "clash of civilizations" and replace it with a different narrative about a war or conflict, not between Islam and the West, but *within* the religion of Islam. The "war" within Islam is fought between and among those who distort Islam's true, authentic, essential meaning and those "moderates" who represent what the religion "really means." The true threats to security thus arise not from "religion" or "Islam" in general, but rather from distorted interpretations of the *essence* of Islam, an Islam whose true meaning is eternal and unchanging.

Underpinning Western state discourse about Islam is a deeper discourse about religion. In all three cases I examine in this book, national security is linked to the triumph of real, authentic religion over "pseudo religion," or religion as ideology—religious faith twisted to suit strategic or political ends. Pseudo religion is posited as a threat to the successful emergence of *real* religion, whose core values and ethics coincide with a variety of liberal tenets such as secularism, toleration, freedom, citizenship, and democracy. The security of the Western secular state thus requires that real religion—embodied in "moderate" Islam—be promoted and protected as a referent object for security. In each case I examine, the state understood itself to have an important role to play in this process.

To be sure, moderate Islam is not an invention of Western governments. There have been and continue to be voices in the Islamic tradition that are liberal or moderate in the political sense I mean it here and that explicitly understand themselves as such. Islamic thinkers of the past, particularly in the mid-19th and early 20th century *nahda* movement, for example, experimented with a Western-style "Reformation" of thought as a way to break free of Western influence (Abu Rabi 1996). Even these reformist movements took place "under the stimulus of European liberal thought," which opened many fruitful intellectual vistas and helped to lay the foundations of Arab secular nationalism (Hourani 1983, 344). What one might call moderate or liberal Islam has continued to be elaborated in different ways by contemporary figures such as Mohammed Arkoun, Abdullah An-Naim, Tariq Ramadan, and Bassam Tibi. Within the liberal or moderate strains of the tradition there is rich variation (Lapidus 2002; Hunter 2009). Intellectual variety is accompanied by geographical diversity. Strong traditions of modernist, moderate, or liberal Muslim thought exist as well in Indonesia and the Philippines for example, two important case studies in this book (Esposito 1987; Sukma and Joewono 2007).

To reiterate, then, I do not claim that Western political elites invented the category of moderate Islam ex nihilo, or that the phrase corresponds to no underlying intellectual or sociological reality. I do claim however that since 9/11, Western secular states have encouraged the development of these religious categories as part of their national security strategies. Classifications such as moderate or liberal Islam serve a strategic function for the Western state. Moderate Islam plays a central role in British, French, and American attempts to counter the ideological threat posed by distortions of the "real" and "essential" religious elements upon which the Western neoliberal world order depends. To safeguard the future of that order Western secular states must take sides in Islam's internal war. Promoting reform in the religion of Islam for purposes of national security lies at the core of a larger post–9/11 phenomenon that I call, building on the Copenhagen School of Securitization Theory, the "securitization of religion."[2]

Securitization Theory, a theory of security, provides the most useful tools with which to capture the post–9/11 relationship between religion and national security and explain its variations and effects. In contrast to theoretical perspectives, which claim that the object of security studies is self-evidently the "study of the threat, use, and control of military force" (Walt 1991), securitization theory suggests that security is a speech-act (Waever 1995; Buzan, Waever, and de Wilde 1998). In other words, relevant actors, typically political elites, frame certain phenomena as a grave threat to something else deemed worth protecting. Once a phenomenon is "securitized" (i.e., framed as a threat), out-of-the ordinary measures are often justified to counter it.

Securitization theory thus involves the study of discourse. I maintain in this book that the securitization of religion—how states encourage religious reform in the name of national security—is first and foremost a discursive phenomenon. At multiple points I show how political officials understood the situation this way themselves, and that part of the strategy to deal with religion is itself discursive. Given that the securitization of religion is predominantly a discursive phenomenon, I adopt the methodology of Discourse Analysis. I examine the public speeches of heads of state, as well as national security strategies for connections elites make between religion and national security. This allows a structured mapping of elite discourse on religion and national security that I perform in chapter 2. I also draw on state documents and policy papers, hearing minutes, newspaper reports, private bilateral correspondences, a large number of U.S. embassy cables and internal memos, and a series of interviews conducted for this book. Through this wide range of sources I show the construction of a more or less coherent discourse about religion and security that Britain, France, and the U.S. all shared after 9/11. This discourse is interesting and important in its own right, but it is also critical to understand because it framed and guided the concrete policies that each state took toward religion.

The general discursive framework that Britain, France, and the U.S. shared regarding religion and national security translated into similar policies such as incorporating references to religion and Islam in counterterrorism and deradicalization programs, training police and security forces in what Islam "really means," promoting targeted outreach to Muslim communities, (re)training religious leaders in secular, liberal values, and perhaps most importantly, establishing or cultivating relationships with "reliable" Muslim representative organizations. Details differ among the cases of course, but there is much overlap. All of these programs were designed to encourage the development of Islam's authentic voices and promote the emergence of a global civil religion more in line with secular liberal priorities. Britain,

France, and the U.S. all concentrated their efforts on encouraging religious reform in the name of national and international security and gaining the support of religious allies in delivering their national security agendas. Such policies are indeed out of the ordinary for three Western states for whom secularism, whether Judeo-Christian or *laicist,* remains at the core of their national identity (Hurd 2008).

Given the similarities in both the discourses and policies of these three states, one might reasonably expect to see similar outcomes. Yet the outcomes were very different. Britain and France have been forced to temper their policies or in some cases even drop them altogether. In Britain, after widespread resistance from a number of Muslim leaders, organizations, and other civil society groups, the state has abandoned programs that sought to both promote national security and community cohesion through religion simultaneously. Attempts to engage in imam training in a coordinated way have largely fallen apart, and coalitions of Muslim representative organizations meant to serve as interlocutors between the British state and the country's Muslim communities have failed to materialize. In France, imam-training programs have not gained the level of support and participation hoped for, while large Muslim representative organizations such as the *Conseil Francais du Culte Musulman* (CFCM) continue to be hampered by internal tensions over legitimacy, fair representation, and the perception that such bodies are meant to be de facto security organs for the French state. The cases of Britain and France thus share a number of features in common. In both cases state alliances with religious representative organizations in order to promote moderate Islam in the name of national security have failed to garner the support hoped for. In both cases, promotion of a certain interpretation of the religion of Islam is widely seen as a mark of loyalty or political obligation, causing much resentment in civil society. Many accuse the state of attempting to manipulate religion for its own strategic ends. Indeed, in Britain and France, state-led attempts to securitize religion appear to have faltered.

In the case of the United States, however, there are increasing calls in the foreign policy, security, and think-tank communities to move ever further toward engaging religious actors abroad in the name of national security. Muslim outreach efforts have expanded in combination with development programs and democracy promotion; U.S. efforts to work with moderate Muslim groups or organizations have intensified through official, bilateral channels; more and more, influential policymakers and think tanks in the U.S. security community are pressing for aggressive promotion of international religious freedom as a matter of national security. But perhaps the most important feature of the post–9/11 U.S. securitization of religion abroad is the use of moderate Islam to help shore up state-to-state alliances with countries such as Indonesia and the Philippines. Finally, in contrast to Britain and France, the U.S. seems poised to expand its "securitizing moves" regarding religion through the increasing incorporation of religion in the defense and military sectors under the rubric of "smart power."

Why, despite clear similarities across the three cases of securitization of religion, have European programs faced far greater obstacles than the U.S. programs? Why have Britain and France scaled back their attempts to securitize religion, while the U.S. seeks to expand it? The difference that makes a difference, I argue, lies in domestic versus international levels of securitization. Securitization theory acknowledges that securitizations (or attempts at securitization) can cut across different levels of analysis. However, in classical securitization theory, levels of analysis are employed as a theoretical heuristic to help ensure that securitization analyses are structured and coherent (Buzan, Waever, and de Wilde 1998, especially 5–7, 17–18). In a globalized world, particularly one in which phenomena are rarely exclusively domestic or international but *transnational,* the distinction between the domestic and international levels of analysis is not always clear. In the empirical portions of this book, however, I argue that levels of analysis remains crucial as a way to help explain why attempted securitizations are more likely to succeed or fail.

Domestically, Britain and France sought to protect their citizens from "distorted" interpretations of religion and Islam by enacting policies that targeted their minority Muslim populations. Such policies conflated "real" Islam with matters of national identity. Because the divide between distorted and authentic Islam was framed in liberal terms—as acceptance or rejection of secularism, freedom, democracy—some Muslim communities viewed the policies as intrusions of the state into matters of faith. In effect, one's loyalty to the state came to be seen as contingent on accepting a certain interpretation of one's religion. As the state encouraged the formation of new representative organizations such as the Sufi Muslim Council in Britain or the CFCM in France, this only exacerbated tensions between and among Muslim representative organizations, their constituents, and the larger civil society in the wake of 9/11. Mohammed Abdul Bari, a prominent leader among the Muslim Council Britain, observed that the state viewed the country's Muslim communities only through "the prism of security" (Abdul Bari 2008). By targeting minority groups, conflating real Islam with elements of the national identity, and placing heavy expectations on Muslim organizations to advance the national security agenda by promoting moderate Islam, Britain and France both faced various forms of backlash and resistance from their internal populations, to whom these governments are accountable.

The United States, meanwhile, has taken measures to securitize religion internationally. The core of this effort involves strengthening state-to-state alliances to help bring religion and Islam into counterterrorism work. The U.S. does this by embarking on programs to protect moderate Muslims abroad from distortions of Islam that could potentially radicalize the global Muslim population and threaten U.S. security and strategic interests. Because the targeted groups live outside of the U.S., the American identity, for example, the notion of an "Islam of America" has little bearing on the content of the discourse and the policy. In contrast to Britain and France, the U.S. has been able to build upon a preexisting network of international bilateral alliances to effect this securitization of religion. This precludes the need to form close, and often controversial, relationships with certain domestic representative Muslim organizations over others, or having to create new partners in executing the security agenda. In fact, states like the Philippines and Indonesia have officially requested that the U.S. play a behind-the-scenes role in promoting reform within Islam.

Attempts by the United States, Britain, and France to encourage reform in Islam as a matter of national security should first be seen as a whole, and then in comparative perspective. The three cases share some similarities but also differ in important and interesting ways. First and most obviously, the United States is not accountable to the global Muslim population, and so any form of resistance or contestation over policy would not require an immediate reassessment of those policies, as it did in Britain and France. Second, because Britain and France brought matters of religion in to their security policies at the domestic level, the referent object for security—real or authentic Islam—was equated with what it means to be a loyal citizen of these countries and partake in the national identity. This became a source of much contestation between the state, Muslim representative organizations, and the Muslim populations these organizations claimed to represent. Finally, the United States did not have to create new Muslim representative organizations to act as "securitizing actors" but was able to make use of preexisting alliances with states in Asia and the Middle East. These states already had in place structures to support the interpretation of Islam along lines amenable to U.S. strategic interests. This has allowed the U.S. to begin expanding its securitization of religion into the defense and the military sectors, and possibly beyond.

From this comparative analysis of the securitization of religion by Britain, France, and the United States, important distinctions can be drawn to contribute to securitization theory as an analytical framework. First, and most obviously, domestic level securitizations run the risk of alienating populations to which states are accountable; states that securitize internationally might not run this same risk. Second, while securitization does appear to result in an us-versus-them dynamic, the risk of alienation is greater at the domestic level. This is because in domestic-level securitizations by the state, certain referent objects such as religion require redefinition along the contours of national identity, attaching them to questions of political obligation, thus making them ripe for contestation and resistance. In contrast, international-level securitizations can make use of preexisting alignments, allowing states to avoid creating unnecessary divisions that further jeopardize their legitimacy. Thus while the general *logic* of securitization holds regardless of the level of analysis at which the scholar operates, states face different sets of obstacles at domestic and international levels when they make securitizing moves. The differences between domestic and international contexts for securitization are significant. Moreover, religion cannot always be conceptualized as an independent variable in international affairs. Religion is itself a contested category in international politics, and nowhere is this more evident than when secular states incorporate matters of religion into their discourses and policies of security.

OUTLINE OF THE BOOK

In the first chapter, I clarify the meaning of central terms that appear throughout this book such as *securitization* and *securitization of religion*. Following this, I place the securitization of religion in historical perspective and end the chapter by developing the anti-essentialist approach to religion I take in this book. It is important to see religion in this way, because how religion is conceptualized by both the state and the academy is itself part of the contemporary practice of security. Taken together, the two arguments of this chapter—one about security, the other about religion—suggest that scholarship on religion in international affairs remains relatively insulated from approaches to security such as securitization theory, and explains why this separation is no longer warranted.

Chapter 2 offers a structured analysis of elite discourse on security, religion, and Islam in Britain, France, and the United States. The chapter highlights a general way of relating religion to national security that the three cases share in common. I focus on the discourses of George W. Bush, Tony Blair, and Nicolas Sarkozy at the macro level: foreign policy speeches, addresses to relevant audiences, and national security documents. All of these macro-level discourses share some key features: first, the notion of a clash of civilizations is replaced with a "war" within Islam, and the security of the Western world order is contingent upon winning it. Second, in this war, the forces of true, moderate Islam represent not only the ideas of Western liberalism but also true religion—what religion really means. Finally, ideological allies must be sought with religious actors in help win the global war of ideas, as national and international security is linked to successful reform in Islam. Thus, post–9/11 British, French, and U.S. discourses each posit authentic, or essential, or moderate Islam as referent objects for security and each envisions a role for the state in encouraging the development of these referent objects.

The empirical chapters of this book—chapters 3, 4, and 5—explore how this elite, macro-level discourse on religion and security translates into three different contexts. Chapters 3 and 4 cover the British and French cases, respectively. Following 9/11 and especially 7/7, the British government adopted quite aggressive policies of counterradicalization justified by the links between religion, security, and community cohesion.[3] Widespread resistance from civil society followed, as a variety of organizations resented the mixing of religion with issues of national security, chafed under the state's categories of moderate and radical Islam, and were harshly critical of state-led efforts to promote certain interpretations of religion over others. In the wake of such resistance the British government attempted to desecuritize religion by ending some programs altogether and definitively separating state-led programs to encourage community cohesion through religion from those aimed at increasing national security.

In chapter 4, I recount the French experience. I explore how President Nicolas Sarkozy attempted to bring religion into the public sphere in France through his concept of positive *laicite,* which helped to justify the close connection between the state, religion, and national security. As in Britain, civil society in France, especially Muslim organizations, resisted the intrusion of the secular state into religious matters, resented the way in which religious interpretation was linked to political obligation, and feared state manipulation of religious belief. Together, chapters 3 and 4 demonstrate that in

Britain and France, backlash from Muslim communities forced the state to abandon or scale back its attempts to securitize religion. Thus I argue that both cases are examples of when securitization of religion fails.

Chapter 5 examines the American case. The U.S. enacted strategies for religious engagement similar to those of Britain and France following 9/11. However, with the help of its bilateral alliances with countries such as the Philippines, Indonesia, and others, the U.S. has largely been able to avoid the problems that Britain and France faced in its securitization of religion. Unlike Britain and France, the U.S. was able to rely on its state allies to act as faithful securitizing partners. The U.S. is also expanding its securitization of religion in an increasing number of sectors under the rubric of "smart power." To appreciate the scope of this growing securitization of religion by the U.S. one should take a wider view of the "security community" in the United States, and this includes not only the military, public officials, and policymakers, and influential think tanks, but also the academic network that produces knowledge about religion. Through discursive analysis and personal interviews, I examine the process by which the U.S. is expanding the securitization of religion both at home and abroad, and the controversies this is generating in U.S. diplomatic and policy circles.

The book's concluding chapter reviews the findings from the case studies and revisits the importance of differentiating between domestic- and international-level securitizations. I elaborate on how a levels-of-analysis approach provides a way to apply securitization theory in comparative perspective and to distinguish between "success" and "failure" outside of a normative framework. My analysis thus has some bearing on whether securitization theory requires a normative component to be analytically useful (Huysmans 2002; Aradau 2004). Finally, turning my attention back to religion, I suggest that the securitization of religion tests the limits of secularism. Securitizing moves regarding religion can place states under pressure to suspend secularism for reasons of national security. Interestingly, this can lead to a paradoxical process of reentrenchment in civil society as religious groups seek to defend secularism anew out of fear of state manipulation of religion. The securitization of religion reveals rich terrain indeed for further theoretical and comparative analysis.

1 ✦ Religion and International Security
Theory and Method

In this chapter I lay out the theoretical and methodological assumptions about religion and security that I bring to this book. I first explain the basic framework of securitization theory and then elaborate what I mean by the "securitization of religion." Following this discussion, I draw on history, sociology of religion, and religious studies to develop further the antiessentialist conception of religion that informs and underpins the book's case studies.

SECURITIZATION THEORY: BASIC COMPONENTS

According to securitization theory, an actor, often but not necessarily a member of the political elite, makes a deliberate choice to frame an issue as a security issue (Buzan, Waever, and de Wilde 1998). The way in which we often think about security—as a noun that denotes a sector of the state apparatus, or as an objective condition—is thus transformed into a verb: securitiza*tion*. Security becomes something than an actor *does*. As Buzan, Waever, and de Wilde write, "security is thus a self-referential practice, because it is in this practice that an issue becomes a security issue—not necessarily because a real existential threat exists but because the issue is presented as a threat" (24). Raising an issue to the level of security can help the agent announcing the security situation to justify taking emergency measures. Such measures might include bending or breaking laws that apply in normal times, or circumventing established political procedures.

This basic structure of the security utterance—whereby something is posited as an existential threat to a referent object—admits of much variation. The enunciating actors, the threats, the referent objects, and the measures taken to deal with threat vary widely according to sector (economic, military) or country, region, political system, or social context. There is also a large amount of what one might call ontological variation in the theory. For example, the referent object—the phenomenon to be protected from threat—can range from tangible (a body, a species, a building complex, an army, the Antarctic) to the intangible (a way of life, a tradition, a collective identity, a set of ideas). The referent object may even be some composite of both, such as the economy, which consists of both tangible (banks) and intangible elements (public confidence). Threats, too, can vary widely in this sense, from the tangible (missiles) to the intangible (a threatening ideology). Finally, securitizing actors—the ones who publicly announce the security situation—may be heads of state, cabinet secretaries, nongovernmental organizations, corporations, activists, protestors, rebels, religious authorities, media personalities, or others. All of these actors are capable of publicly presenting a security argument, and all of them do. Thus, securitization has a common logic but many variations.

Securitizations do more than posit threats. Discourses do not simply describe reality but play a role in constructing it, and security discourse is no different (see, for example, Campbell 1992; also Hansen 2006). Taken-for-granted ways of categorization and classification of the world help shape collective understanding of what can legitimately count as an object of scientific analysis (Foucault 1970). Discourse can shape the meanings of things, or help to bring into being phenomena that then come to be taken as real. In his classic 1989 study of myth, discourse, and classification for example, Bruce Lincoln showed how the effect of imperial discourses transformed the consciousness of colonized peoples so that they "came to consider themselves members of an imperial society rather than the vanquished subjects of a foreign nation" (Lincoln 1989, 4). Discourse thus constructs *social* meanings and can even lead to new modes of self-understanding and collective identity. Securitization theory holds generally this about what a community considers a "threat," as well as what it considers worth protecting. Naming threats and referent objects helps bring *both* into being. This is why the analysis of discourse is so important in any study of securitization.

Following 9/11, Western secular governments have gone to great lengths to encourage the construction of moderate Islam in order to protect national security. In fact, the referent object moderate Islam is meant to bring into being the phenomena it intends to objectively describe. As one former Bush administration official put it, the United States' 2006 National Security Strategy introduced the concept of moderate Islam and hoped that reformist Muslims would "populate that category" (Inboden 2012). Whether the people on the receiving end of this securitization recognize themselves in this category is a different story, however. In fact, as I demonstrate in the following chapters, the religious categories encouraged by the state may find little purchase with religious communities, contributing to securitization's failure.

The Securitization of Religion

By the "securitization of religion," I refer to the post–9/11 attempts by Western, secular states to engage with religious actors and ideas for reasons of national security. At the core of this engagement lies state-led attempts to encourage the development of certain interpretations of religion—especially Islam—over others. Indeed, for all three of the states examined in this book, reforming Islam became a national security priority in the wake of 9/11. In the specialized language of securitization theory, one might say that after 9/11, "authentic religion," what religion "really means," and the "real meaning" of Islam have become *referent objects* for security: something to be protected from threat. According to political elites, the threat to real religion comes from distortions, radical perversions of religion, or "pseudo religious" ideologies that prey on the young, the vulnerable, and the weak of faith.

I am not the first scholar to attempt to theorize what one might call the securitization of religion or to look at religion through the lens of securitization theory. To begin with, religion does play a role, albeit a small one, in the original theory of securitization. Most often, religion is presented as a potential referent object in the societal sector of security, the sector in which a society takes its collective identity as a referent object for security (Buzan, Waever, and de Wilde 1998, 23). Buzan, Waever, and de Wilde speculate other "statelike" or "state-paralleling" organizations can serve as referent objects in the post–Cold War world, including "transnational movements" that "are able to mobilize supreme allegiance from adherents" such as "some world religions" (145). When discussing the military sector, the authors note that "Western fears of Islam, the rise of Hindu nationalism, and theories

about the 'clash of civilizations'" continue to animate discussion in the post–
Cold War climate, which suggests that "the Westphalian state's claims to
exclusivity as the referent object for military security" is no longer beyond
question 53).

Later work in securitization theory takes a closer look at religion (Laustsen and Waever 2003). Arguing that following the end of the Cold War "the
roots of conflicts are increasingly related to culture and identity," Laustsen
and Waever wish to "explore the logic of securitization of objects that are
clearly of a religious nature" (148). They examine religion as a referent object
for security by first isolating "the religious element in religion," emphasizing how actors not only look to their faith for security but, as we see in the
case of Al Qaeda and others, take measures to secure their "true faith" from
what they deem as corrosive, existential threats. More recent work applies
securitization theory to the European experience with religion, especially
Islam. Jocelyn Cesari, referring to the "securitization of Islam," focuses on
changes to European immigration policy and antidiscrimination measures
(Cesari 2009). Kaya Ayhan applies securitization theory to contemporary
regimes of migration and integration in Europe and approaches religion
in this context (Ayhan 2012). The construction of Muslim immigration as
a national security threat by the state conjures an aura of collective fear,
distracting from the deeper reality that heightened religious identity claims
result from existing structural problems in the European project. The more
migration is treated in the public sphere as a matter of national security,
the deeper the cycle of exclusion and antagonism, causing younger gen-
erations to revisit and revise the religion(s) of their parents to help anchor
their identities (185). In another recent work, Stuart Croft examines the
"securitization of Islam" in Britain (Croft 2012). Croft traces the evolution
of what it means to be "British" and how today, 'Britishness' is constructed
"in contradistinction to a new Islamist terrorist Other" (2). Croft expands
on securitization theory to move beyond the level of the state and political elites to capture how British national identity provides a "resource of
security" for individuals and how the "everyday lives" of Britons have been
affected and even "reconstructed" by the framing of Islam as a threat (2). In
contrast to this recent work, I too focus on religion but concentrate instead
on how *states* grapple with religion as a matter of national security. Looking
at the situation this way helps to make sense of the increasing tendency of
states to link religion and security together in the post–9/11 world, efforts
that translate into actual policies that one U.S. think tank provocatively
called "religion building" (Benard 2003).

Religion and Securitization: Historical and
Conceptual Foundations

State attempts to channel the development of religion into certain acceptable pathways in the name of national security date back to the birth of the modern state system. In the post–Reformation period a new concept of religion was "being born . . . one of domesticated belief systems," which were "insofar as possible, to be manipulated by the sovereign for the benefit of the state" at the time when newly emerging states were competing with each other for survival (Cavanaugh 1995, 405; see also Molnar 2002). Even the word religion (*religio*) itself bears the marks of state power, as European territorial princes deployed the term strategically to invoke common moralities and a collective sense of political obligation to guard against insecurity, civil disorder, and social upheaval. At the core of the new notion of religion, embodied in the Magisterial Reformation, lay an ingredient of "control from within that was thought necessary for peaceful political life" and obedience to earthly political power (Molnar 2002, 59). Foucault would later reveal the connections between new notions of religion as discipline and (self)-policing and the "explosion" of questions of governmentality in the aftermath of the Reformation and the wars of religion (Foucault 1991, 87).

In a way that parallels today, early modern states claimed for themselves the "right to reform" religion (*jus reformandi*) to protect from insecurity and chaos (Blaschke 1996, 67). Emerging secular powers took a keen interest in religious doctrine because theology was a way to justify and cement political obligation and achieve security. In Germany, in the aftermath of the first wave of the Reformation, religious doctrine was used to solidify state control and protect against both international and external threats. As one scholar puts it, "religion . . . was the best instrument to produce the voluntary obedience of subjects to princes and to establish harmony between the different estates and social classes" (Schilling 1986, 24). In exercising its right to reform religion the early modern state also assumed responsibility for religious education, including the training of pastors and the formation of representative religious organizations to the state. It also expected formal confessions of faith from its subjects, for the new religious energies unleashed by the Reformation could not be left to develop on their own. Indeed, early modern European states took a keen interest in channeling the religious direction of the Reformation and sought to link political loyalty to religious commitment. Again, in the German territories, where competition among emerging territorial states was greatest, "the confession of faith in the

Lutheran territorial church was also a confession of loyalty to the territorial state" (Blaschke 1996, 72). The early modern principle of *cuius regio, eius religio* ("the ruler determines the religion of his realm"), expressed in the 1555 Peace of Augsburg, encapsulated this process by which the state attempted to direct and channel religious change by tying religious belief and political obligation together as a matter of security.

Later, Enlightenment political thought attacked the foundations of Christian political theology, seeking to ground the political in autonomous human reason (Lilla 2007). Nonetheless, religion was never far from the minds of thinkers such as Hobbes, Locke, and Kant. For Rousseau, religion played a crucial role in maintaining social and political solidarity, necessary for the exercise of the general will. Rousseau termed this "civil religion." Such a civil religion imagined an "ethical community which integrates all citizens into a political cult coextensive with the political community and competing allegiances to either more primordial or more universalistic forms of community" (Casanova 1994, 59). While the general intellectual tendency of Enlightenment thought sought to free politics from transcendental justification and theological speculation, the state still had a role to play in encouraging religious bonds between and among its subjects and citizens. The phenomenon we see today—the involvement of the Western state with matters of religion—thus has an extended historical precedent, dating from the very beginnings of European modernity.

Religion also played a crucial role in the projection of European power on a global scale. As rising European powers encountered their colonial subjects, new conceptual categories were needed to define beliefs, rituals, and behaviors considered foreign and strange to the Judeo-Christian tradition. Hinduism, for example, may well have been a construction of British colonial interests, as the colonizer needed some way to classify and hence control a massive and complex tapestry of people and traditions (see B. K. Smith 1989). There is a sense then in which Europe's intellectual categories such as Hinduism and others are themselves political; they assist in reproducing systems of colonial and neocolonial control but at the same time serve to distort understanding of others outside of the Anglo-European area (Asad 1993).

Even our very concept of world religions took shape in a wider geopolitical context of tremendous insecurity in Europe. As Tomoko Masuzawa has shown, the concept of world religions arose between World Wars I and II, a period in which Anglo-European scholars and governments, internalizing a sense of crisis, came to feel that "one should want to acquire, and acquire quickly, a sweeping knowledge of the multiplicity of religions in the world because a new techno-geopolitics was unfolding dramatically before one's eyes" (Masuzawa 2005, 41). Reacting to these emerging perceptions of global interconnectedness that left the state vulnerable and insecure, the idea of world religious traditions were born of a need to reclaim some semblance of order in and control over the international system. Indeed, those traditions that have come to be consolidated into "world religions" refer to social forms originating outside of the Anglo-European project that have at one time or another arisen to balance the power of "the West."

> It is impossible to escape the suspicion that a world religion is . . . above all, a tradition that has achieved sufficient power and numbers to enter our history to form it, interact with it, or thwart it. We recognize both the unity within and the diversity among the world religions because they correspond to geopolitical entities with which we must deal. (J. Z. Smith 1998, 280)

The contemporary incorporation of religion into the security discourse and practices of Western states should be seen within this larger histori-cal and conceptual context. From the rise and consolidation of the early modern state in the wake of the Reformation, political power has sought to influence the development and trajectory of religion in the name of security, obedience, and order. This may require forays into religious thought or even theological or doctrinal disputes, because in times of heightened insecurity and crisis, states are apt to draw distinctions between what counts as religion and what does or should not. Even for secular states, religions can become hermeneutic battlegrounds, as "ideas become more malleable and are used strategically to promote and legitimate a particular vision at the expense of others" (Williams 1996, 371). In periods of insecurity and unease, the secular state turns again to the religious sphere.

Theological or doctrinal debates can be directed by the state into ac-ceptable channels to help demarcate the boundaries of political obligation, as when, in the wake of the Protestant Reformation, emerging territorial powers in Europe helped to shape new understandings of religion under conditions of acute insecurity and competition. We can, for example, see a similar relationship between conceptions of religion and national secu-rity in the United States. The notion that religion has a unique sui generis existence—that religion is utterly otherworldly, internal, and spiritual, a notion that many Americans grow up with—became collective "common sense" not during one of the country's religious awakenings, but during the Cold War, as the U.S. competed with the Soviet Union for global hegemony. During that time of existential insecurity, religious education was part of the nation's political socialization, for religious faith made for strong, resilient communities and was a mark of democratic citizenship, national spiritual vitality, and superiority over atheistic communism. As one scholar argues, "the reinvention of the confessional (largely Protestant) study of religion as a Humanistic discipline eligible for tax dollars cannot adequately be understood apart from the context provided by the Cold War" (McCutcheon 2004a, 45). Political power, national security imperatives, and sites of intellectual and cultural production can thus mutually reinforce each other. Religion is, at least in part, a complex of ideas, categories, and classifications embedded in the security practices of the nation. What lesson should we draw from such historical considerations? Simply that religion and what it refers to cannot be taken for granted, for various ways of understanding and defining religion and religious traditions have political implications. This is what makes religion so contentious a referent object for security. Conceptually, it is therefore necessary to always question whether religion is "so obviously an ontologically distinct part of the human condition" (McCutcheon 2004b, 171).

It should be noted that such an antiessentialist approach to religion goes further than methodological agnosticism regarding what "religion" means. It is not simply my intention to claim that religion can be defined in many ways. Religion can indeed be defined in many ways—at least 50, according to one source (J. Z. Smith 1998). Religion is notoriously difficult to define, and this too has long been recognized. In the very first sentence of his landmark *Sociology of Religion,* Max Weber writes that "to define religion, to say what it is, is not possible at the start of a presentation such as this . . . definition can be attempted, if at all, only at the conclusion of the study" (Weber 1963, 1). The conceptual strategy of this book, however, is not to hazard a definition of religion at the conclusion of the empirical research. It is rather to examine religion's embeddedness in the contemporary discourse and practice of security, recognizing that various conceptions of "religion" themselves have become part of the post–9/11 security complex. The two terms—religion and security—thus have something in common; namely, a performative element whereby both are given social meaning in the process of talking about and dealing with them. What either term refers to is the result of a process; in this case, an ongoing process in which political elites struggle to balance familiar elements of security such as surveillance and coercive power with conceptual, ideational elements that have traditionally been seen as foreign to security discourse and practice. This is what it means to say that religion has no self-evident or sui generis meaning, and scholars should not approach the study of religion in global politics assuming that it does. To do so would render religion as something "overly mysterious" (Nexon 2011, 160) and miss the ways in which religion is tied in more and more with the politics of security in the present era.

Traditional modes of security theorizing in global politics do not capture the intersection between religion and security as well as one that problematizes religion from the outset. Realist theories of security, for example, argue generally that threats exist independently outside of an actor's talking about them. If the main issue for security studies is war, for example, then what security scholars should be studying is the "threat, use, and control of military force" (Walt 1991, 212). The referent object for realist security studies remains the territorial integrity of the sovereign state and the physical safety of the people who live there. With the exception of a particular brand of Christian realism, if religion has been relevant at all from the realist perspective it is as an ideology that may under certain circumstances drive actors to cooperate or to conflict. Yet there is no necessary reason for religion to be absent from the realist theoretical framework. Even in its most traditional structuralist variants realism need not be deficient at all in taking religious factors into account. Religion can help order, disorder, or even reorder the international system, alter the global balance of power, or shape the behavior of the system's units (Snyder 2011). Constructivism, too, can accommodate religion easily given that approaches' traditional focus on transnational actors and processes, and the domestic determinants of national identity and foreign policy (Snyder 2011; Katzenstein 2006). Constructivists indeed tend to focus on religion as part of the background culture against which states operate (Thomas 2006). From the constructivist perspective, religion, like other cultural factors, can be causal in the loose sense that it can help to form the "identities, and hence the security interests, of states" (Katzenstein 1996, 2). All states, no matter the level of material or military security they enjoy, are embedded in larger cultural or institutional environments that impact the national identity and the state's conception of what is in its national interest.

In conclusion, to study the securitization of religion requires the scholar to leave behind the assumption that religion is singly an independent variable that influences the behavior of actors for good or ill. Religion is also much more than a matter of background culture or collective social tradition. Neither reducible to material factors such as class interest nor wholly ideational, one can study religion as a vehicle through which states attempt to define and shape collective identities and practices, maintain the boundaries of political obligation, and form alliances for national security. These require both discursive and policy processes that, like any securitization in a democratic society, can be accepted, contested, or resisted by civil society. The securitization of religion is thus a relational process of construction of religion as a referent object—a push and pull between the state and religious communities. Discourse analysis is a particularly appropriate method for studying religion in international affairs in this way, for it is attuned to the ways in which systems of framing and categorization construct and constitute social realities. A securitization approach thus takes the very constitution of religion by the political-intellectual establishment as its subject matter, capturing the performative element that religion and security share.

The Securitization of Religion and Levels of Analysis

I would now like to provide more detail about how this book contributes to securitization theory as a whole. The securitization of religion—post–9/11 attempts by Western states to engage with religious ideas and actors for reasons of national security—has both discursive and policy components. All three cases examined in this book share the same basic discourse about religion and Islam. Political elites in Britain, France and the U.S. in the wake of 9/11 all sought to undermine the "clash of civilizations" thesis by positing a war or clash within Islam instead of a clash between Islam and the West. Although Britain, France, and the U.S. adopted similar discourse and policies, however, the outcomes were very different. I argue that levels of analysis play a crucial role in such cases of relative success or failure.

In the classic early approach to securitization theory, Buzan, Waever, and de Wilde suggested that "levels are simply ontological referents for where things happen rather than sources of explanation in themselves" (1998, 5). In other words, levels of analysis themselves have no explanatory power. However, the cases in this book demonstrate that religion as a referent object for security has very different consequences at different levels of analysis. At the domestic level of analysis, the referent object for security—moderate or authentic versions of the religion of Islam—is attached to other signifiers such as British-Muslim or French-Muslim identity. This process, known in discourse analysis as the process of *articulation* is an example of how "chains of connotations are established between different linguistic elements by which meaning is created and temporarily fixed" (Fierke 2007, 85). In this case, moderate Islam is one crucial point in a larger web of descriptions, identity designations, and all of the expectations and obligations they imply. Moderate Islam is a complicated referent object, suggesting a way of interpreting the religion that not only eschews violence but stays silent on contentious issues of foreign policy as well. Moreover, *moderation* comes to refer to a religious individual or community whose ideas, beliefs, opinions, and identities are nonthreatening and loyal to the state. When interpretations of religion are linked to matters of political obligation to the nation or the state, they are often looked upon with suspicion by religious communities. This was the case, for example, in Britain and France, and is one reason why religion failed as a referent object for security at this domestic level.

Domestic-level securitizations of religion are difficult for secular states to undertake because perceived security imperatives tempt states to venture beyond their widely accepted limits regarding religion and push into the realm of ideas. This is treacherous terrain for the secular state and in such cases the state requires trustworthy allies in civil society to help it legitimate the terms according to which increased engagement with religious actors and ideas will take place. As the state reaches out to religious actors in the hope of forming alliances for security, many religious actors in civil society come to feel that their acceptance as full, respected citizens in the national society is made conditional upon how effective they are in assisting the state to bring into being a certain interpretation of their faith. Correct interpretations of religion are transformed from exclusively theological matters into ways to access state resources and patronage. For these reasons, we see in the cases of Britain and France how cracks begin to form in the state's relationship with religious actors until the state's securitization of religion ultimately fails. In Britain, the state thus dropped many of its outreach policies targeting Muslim communities and sought to *desecuritize* religion by definitively separating state programs designed to promote community cohesion from those engaged in domestic security and counterterrorism. In France, religious leaders resented the categories used to describe them and came to see the secular state's intervention into religious affairs as setting a dangerous precedent for increased manipulation of religion by the state for national security purposes.

The U.S. securitization of religion takes place internationally, at the state-to-state level of analysis, where it is conducted under the rubric of "smart power." The U.S. promotes moderate Islam by proxy for a number of purposes, but especially to reinforce flagging alliances in the fight against terrorism. We see this, for example, in the cases of Philippines and Indonesia. In these cases the U.S. diplomatic and military establishment seeks closer cooperation with the foreign state in promoting the development of moderate Islam for security purposes. The U.S. encourages these states to reach out to certain religious organizations and plays a background role in the process of channeling Islam's ideological development. At the international level of analysis the formation of alliances with religious actors in the name of national security appears to be more successful because between the main securitizing power (the U.S.) and the indigenous religious community there is the power of another sovereign state. It falls to this sovereign state to cultivate the alliances with domestic religious actors and to them also falls the task of ensuring that the acceptable referent object (mainstream, moderate Islam) emerges successfully. The foreign state takes upon itself the risk of domestic resistance or backlash.

What do these cases suggest about religion's success or failure as a referent object for security? Mainly that securitizations of religion are more difficult and likely to fail when the secular state is perceived to be the driving force behind the construction of the religious referent object. This is most likely to happen at the domestic level of analysis. It is risky for the secular state to actively encourage a national religious minority to support a certain interpretation of their faith in the name of national security. Such a situation is far more likely to arise at the domestic level of analysis because here access to and acceptance by the wider society is made conditional on accepting a certain interpretation of one's religion. The securitization of religion seems more successful, however, when it is part of a wider attempt to understand, engage, and influence religious actors abroad with the help of state allies. Thus, in contrast to what one might expect from securitization theory, levels of analysis do matter in the case of religion. In fact, it is precisely at the "middle scale of limited collectivities" that religion appears to be a more controversial and difficult referent object for security, not less (Buzan, Waever, and de Wilde 1998, 36). If a referent object must secure the allegiance of a population for a securitization to be counted as "successful," religion fails on precisely this score when it becomes an object of construction by the secular state.

There are other adjustments to securitization theory that are also relevant here. As this book shows, securitization need not always be about breaking rules; securitization can happen "*below* the level of exceptionality" (Stritzel 2007; see also Vuori 2008 and Croft 2012). Though unusual, attempts by Britain, France, and the U.S. to encourage the construction of moderate

Islam as a referent object for security do not signify a drastic step into emergency politics or require the suspension of the law. But these states do place their secular arrangements under stress as they attempt to engage with religion in the public sphere more than ever before. In each case, state engagement with religious ideas and actors in the name of national security tests the limits of received traditions of secularism. Although this may not qualify as a style of emergency politics or the suspension of the law per se, the securitization of religion by Western secular states requires a step outside of the state's settled arrangements with religion. Britain's promotion of moderate Islam and state intervention into theology goes exceeds any institutional arrangement traditionally extended to the Church of England for example. In France, where the state has a long history of engagement with religious groups, Sarkozy's conception of *positive laicite* goes far beyond what has been customary, to the extent that French religious organizations have emerged alongside diehard secularists as the most outspoken critics of positive *laicite*. In the case of the U.S., efforts to promote international religious freedom always raised hackles over the constitutional separation of church and state, but post–9/11 efforts to engage with religious actors abroad to promote certain versions of Islam (especially by the defense establishment) have heightened the intensity of this objection, especially in the diplomatic community.

Thus, securitizations do not always have to be about breaking rules or creating states of exception in order to represent a step outside of the bounds of established practice or the "normal bargaining process" of the political sphere (Buzan, Waever, and de Wilde 1998, 4). This point is crucial because all three states examined in this book did in fact take emergency measures, and in some cases, suspend normal legal procedure to deal with threat in the wake of 9/11. After the bombings of 7/7/05, for example, the British government "argued the need for a change of rules to make it possible to target extremists for deportation" (Fierke 2007, 85; see also Cesari 2009). States did take some extraordinary emergency measures after 9/11. However, this does not give the whole picture, for what remains to be investigated is state discourse and policy surrounding religion per se.

CONCLUSION

For many international relations scholars the history of the rise of the modern state since Westphalia is the central narrative of the discipline. Religion's apparent "return" from its "exile" after 9/11 challenges the discipline's Westphalian assumption that religion should play no role in international politics, understood to consist of relations between and among sovereign states in an anarchical system (Hatzopoulos and Petito 2003). The theoretical perspectives that have so far come to dominate the study of global politics internalized this secularist assumption, leaving them ill-prepared to take into account religions' "global resurgence" in international affairs. Religion can no longer be ignored, however, and so states and scholars alike need to take "religion seriously" in international affairs, lest they fail to see new conflicts coming or miss opportunities for conflict resolution and peacebuilding.

From the perspective of securitization theory, however, the story is somewhat different. Looking back over the development of the state, the securitization scholar does not see a gradually secularizing world order but rather a history of state intervention into religious matters in the name of protecting an emerging referent object from inner and outer chaos and destruction. Neither is religion an independent variable, or a mysterious ideational force that surges once again onto the international political scene in the wake of 9/11. Finally, religion's role in global politics cannot be reduced to either a potent threat to the Westphalian order of states or a moral force that can help usher in a "post-Westphalian period of global coexistence" (Hatzopoulos and Petito 2003). Central to this book is the thesis that religion has no self-evident, universally accepted content, but is rather a mode of classification that political forces use strategically when they perceive the nation to be under threat. From this perspective, it is theoretically more fruitful and empirically more accurate to study how states classify "parts of the observable world as religious in the first place" instead of studying religion as an independent variable that impacts collective or individual behavior (McCutcheon 2004b, 176).

The securitization of religion after 9/11 represents the latest chapter in a long history of the state engaging with religious actors and ideas to handle insecurity, unease, and crisis. According to the evidence I present in this book, Western states have encouraged the development of a particular interpretation of religion, especially Islam, as a central part of their search for security in a post–9/11 world. However, as this book demonstrates, it is a matter of contention whether the secular state should be involved in the process of "religion-building" at all.

2 ✦ Securitization of Religion

The Basic Discourse

In the years following September 11, 2001, George W. Bush, Tony Blair, and Nicolas Sarkozy described what appeared to be a fundamentally altered geopolitical landscape in a similar way. All three leaders converged on the notion that a new "war of ideas" had emerged in which discourse mattered as much if not more than military action. The concept of a war of ideas was not a post–9/11 invention, however. The U.S. national security establishment had used the term during the Cold War to describe its worldwide struggle against Communism, which one U.S. official referred to at the time as "'a 20th century Islam,' a godless faith in modern guise that fought to annihilate the 'foundations of Western civilization'" (Peck 2010, 16, 20). But while U.S. Cold War discourses linked Communism to religion through analogy and metaphor, the post–9/11 war of ideas was for Bush, Blair, and Sarkozy quite literally a global *religious* struggle. A global war was raging between those who embraced true, authentic religious faith as the foundational source of their shared values and identity, and those who would twist, pervert, or "hijack" the teachings of a great world religion, Islam.

In the early 1990s, U.S. scholar Samuel Huntington had predicted a global struggle based primarily on religious identity in his books and articles about a "clash of civilizations" (Huntington 1993). According to Huntington, struggles between and among civilizations will occur in the "fault lines" that separate them and might well prove to be "the battle lines of the future" (1). Foremost among these battles, Huntington predicted, will be the conflict between "the West" on one hand and a monolithic "Islamic civilization" (embodied in the world's "Islamic states") on the other. Though published more than a decade before 9/11, Huntington's notion of a clash of civilizations became a potent and popular way to describe events of that day and their aftermath.

Pundits and scholars worried that if political elites, especially George W. Bush, talked too explicitly about Islam in public this would play into Osama bin Laden's hands and help bring into being the very clash of civilizations the U.S. and its allies should avoid. In fact, the 2002 National Security Strategy of the U.S. makes little mention of Islam or religion. Quickly, however, Bush, along with Tony Blair and Nicolas Sarkozy, incorporated the "clash" discourse into their public speeches as a rhetorical foil, basing their interpretation of the geopolitical situation on precisely the opposite claim: there *is* no clash of civilizations between the West and Islam, all three argued, and those who claim that there is seek to "hijack the teachings of a great religion," in the words of Bush. Bush, Blair, and Sarkozy attempted instead to undermine the notion of the clash of civilizations by replacing Huntington's "clash" with a global war *within* the religion of Islam, positing an intrareligious struggle that implicated the West, threatened its security, and required Western states to take sides. This global, spiritual struggle for the "soul" of a world religion needed the Western, secular state to harness the very power of religion to fight and win it. It was a struggle in which religion was seen as both part of the problem and part of the solution. In other words, if the War on Terror had a religious component, there was no reason why the Western state too could not harness religion as a weapon.

Bush, Blair, and Sarkozy thus sought to short-circuit Huntington's prediction of intercivilizational war by subsumed it under another, very different narrative. In order for the West to be victorious in this spiritual war, and for the global balance of power to be restored, real, authentic religious faith must triumph over false interpretations or distortions of religion. There can, however, be no distortion if there is no authentic original, and so the authentic, original meaning of religion needs to be elaborated as a referent object for security. In a number of foreign policy speeches, all three present us with a vision of just such a referent object, attaching to religion a chain of signifiers that also need to be defended from the existential threat of pseudo-religion. Specifically, "authentic," "real," "modern" religious faith embodies the core ethical principles that all world religions share, especially Islam and Christianity, and coincides with a variety of liberal values such the embrace of secularity, toleration, freedom, citizenship, and democracy. Bush, Blair, and Sarkozy thus construct a complex referent object for security that links together authentic religion, the essence of Islam, and a host of liberal political values. Radical distortions of the *essence* of Islam, of what the religion "really means," threaten the existence of this referent object and, by extension, the Western world order. The Western state must therefore take measures to fortify it and ensure the survival of real religion.

RELIGION AND U.S. NATIONAL SECURITY DISCOURSE

Prior to September 11, 2001, President George W. Bush made a number of references to religion in contexts in which one would expect to hear them: at the inaugural address, the announcement of the Faith-Based and Community Initiative (January 2001), the National Prayer Breakfast (February 2001), the dedication of the Pope John Paul II Cultural Center (March 2001), and a speech on stem cell research (August 2001). During this period Bush tended to tie his "God Talk" (Lincoln 2006) to a few recurring themes: the constructive role that religion can play in charity and poverty alleviation in the United States (a central plank in Bush's vision of Compassionate Conservatism); the sanctity of human life in terms of cloning, stem cell research, abortion; and the importance of religious freedom for healthy democracies. Most of this is, at least for the United States, standard conservative fare.

Following the attacks of 9/11, however, Bush and his staff embarked on a trial-and-error effort to describe and communicate to multiple audiences the threat faced by the United States. Bush's religious discourse quickly evolved new features, the most conspicuous of which was the struggle between good and evil (Bush 2001a; Bush 2001b). On September 14, 2001, for example, Bush gave a speech at the National Day of Prayer and Remembrance in which he reasserts the U.S. determination to "rid the world of evil" (Bush 2001b). Shortly after, Bush elaborated that "the terrorists" are "instruments of evil" and "evil's willing servants" (Bush 2001e). Bush then went on to separate "Islam itself" from perversions of the religion.

This distinction coincides with Bush's first substantial mention of Al Qaeda in the Address to the Joint Session of the 107th Congress in 2001. Here Bush speaks of a "fringe form of Islamic extremism . . . that perverts the peaceful teachings of Islam" (Bush 2001c). "The terrorists," Bush notes, are "traitors to their own faith, trying, in effect, to hijack Islam itself" and who "reject every limit of law, morality, and religion" (Bush 2001c; Bush 2001e). Such terrorists make "pretenses to piety" and are the heirs to the 20th century's "murderous ideologies" and have "abandoned every value except the will to power" (Bush 2001c). The underlying distinction between "Islam itself" and distortions or perversions of it is a central theme that will be repeated with only minor variations by Tony Blair and Nicolas Sarkozy.

This discourse of true versus false Islam and the distinction between religion and ideology that underpins it culminated in Bush's address at the Islamic Center of Washington on September 17, 2001. In this well-known address Bush claimed that the acts of 9/11 "violate the fundamental tenets of the Islamic faith" and that "the face of terror is not the true faith of Islam . . . that's not what Islam is all about. Islam is peace" (Bush 2001d). In his address to the United Nations General Assembly on November 10, 2001, Bush reiterated that same discourse, that "terrorists are violating the tenets of every religion, including the one they invoke" and that they "hide behind Islam" (Bush 2001f).

The theme of real religion—real Islam—versus religion as ideology continued as the War on Terror unfolded. In his remarks on the Freedom Agenda at the U.S. Chamber of Commerce, for example, Bush noted that "groups of men have gained influence in the Middle East and beyond through an ideology of theocratic terror. Behind their language of religion is the ambition for absolute political power" (Bush 2003). Later, in 2005, Bush reiterated the same distinction in a speech to the National Endowment for Democracy: "some call this evil Islamic radicalism; others, militant Jihadism . . . whatever it's called, this ideology is very different from the religion of Islam. This form of radicalism exploits Islam to serve a violent, political vision" (Bush 2005a).

From the aftermath of September 11, 2001, until 2005, Bush thus relies heavily in his public discourse on the distinction between true religion and religion as ideology. It is the use of religion as ideology that distinguishes the radicals who are "obsessed with ambition" and who twist religion in instrumental and tactical ways to "rally the masses" (Bush 2005a). However, while Bush distinguishes between true faith and its perversions and sets the global war on terror in something of a theological-historical narrative during this period, he does not yet explicitly link U.S. national security strategy to the development of moderate versions of Islam or to the formation of ideological alliances.

Nor does religion feature in any extended way in the National Security Strategy of 2002, but the document does introduce the argument about the clash of civilizations that would become a central plank in U.S., British, and French discourse on Islam. The overall focus of the 2002 National Security Strategy is on defusing regional conflicts, preventing the proliferation of weapons of mass destruction (WMDs), global economic growth through free trade and free markets, building "infrastructures of democracy," and other themes. The Strategy does argue that "for most of the twentieth century, the world was divided by a great struggle over ideas: destructive totalitarian visions versus freedom and equality" but "that great struggle is now over" (USNSS 2002, 1). There is now a new "war of ideas" that the U.S. will wage through the effective use of public diplomacy and "supporting moderate and modern government, especially in the Muslim world" in order to ensure that "the conditions and ideologies that promote terrorism do not find fertile ground" (6). Later in the document one finds the key discursive move: "the war on terrorism is not a clash of civilizations. It does, however, reveal the clash *inside* a civilization, a battle for the future of the Muslim world. This is a struggle of ideas and this is an area where America must excel" (31; emphasis mine). Here we have the denial of the clash of civilizations and its replacement by a very different narrative in the U.S. National Security Strategy of 2002. The document lays out the basic idea behind U.S. discourse on religion and Islam that was to emerge in a much more highly elaborated form in the National Security Strategy of 2006.

In the immediate aftermath of 9/11 Bush had emphasized that Islam was a "religion of peace" (Inboden 2011). To suggest otherwise would imply that the U.S. had embarked on a worldwide war against all those who professed the religion of Islam. Bush had made an off-the-cuff comment about the War on Terror as a "crusade," which Osama bin Laden and Ayman al-Zawahiri seized upon and exploited at great length. Bush never used the word crusade again, but the incident taught the U.S. establishment a valuable lesson about controlling its message about religion and Islam in the context of the War on Terror. The problem, however, as one former Bush administration official noted, was that even descriptions of Islam as a "religion of peace" created a conservative blowback at home—Bush was too soft on Islam—and seemed to gain little traction abroad (Inboden 2011). The U.S. had a discursive problem: remarks about a crusade would only heighten the perception of a U.S. war on Islam—reinforcing the very clash of civilizations the administration tried to undermine—but the attacks of 9/11 clearly seemed to the administration to have *some* religious component. The Bush administration needed to carve out a new discursive space to describe the security situation, one that would elaborate a middle ground between the radical options of global religious crusade on one hand, and utter neglect of religion on the other. The National Security Strategy of 2006 attempted to elaborate a new way of framing the relationship between religion and national security.

William Inboden was brought from the State Departments' Policy Plan-

ning staff to the National Security Council to help craft a new National Security Strategy. According to Inboden, the 2006 strategy was to be different:
"there was more willingness to speak in a more detailed way about the role
of Islam in the conflict" than there was in 2002 (Inboden 2011). Inboden
continued, "what we tried to do was on the one hand be honest and realistic
about the ideological and religious nature of the enemy that we faced," a
threat that was widely thought to include "irreducibly religious elements."
On the other hand, "there was a concern that if we say it's a war on anything
inherently Islamic" then "that would elevate the conflict to a war against a
whole religion" (Inboden 2011). "We were speaking to multiple audiences
with this thing," Inboden recalled, including the National Security Council,
the Congress, the American public, and people around the world. The team
was thus quite conscious that "any language we used could be used by the
enemy." In the end, "we decided to treat it (the "jihadist threat") as an ideology with religious components" (Inboden 2011).

Striking a balance between capturing the "irreducibly religious" elements
of the threat without implicating the wider religion of Islam required a
number of distinctions to be drawn. In a section of the 2006 strategy titled
"Strengthening Alliances to Defeat Global Terrorism and Work to Prevent
Attacks Against Us and Our Friends," the document states that "from the
beginning the War on Terror has been both a battle of arms and a battle of
ideas . . . in the long run, winning the war on terror means winning the
battle of ideas . . . while the War on Terror is a battle of ideas, it is not a battle
of religions. The transnational terrorists confronting us today exploit the
proud religion of Islam to serve a violent political vision" (USNSS 2006).

Thus the 2006 National Security Strategy gave far more detail about and
placed much more emphasis than before on the explicitly religious dimensions of the global War on Terror. After 2006, the concept of a "war of ideas"
became the new, overarching framework for the national security strategy of
the United States as Bush increasingly began to refer in public to a global
struggle taking place within Islam. A new discursive space had been found:
the United States must take sides in the war within Islam by supporting
moderate, mainstream versions of Islam in the name of national and international security. As Inboden remarked, "we created this thing called moderate Islam and we hoped Muslim reformers would come to inhabit this space"
(Inboden 2011).

The 2006 National Security Strategy not only moved the war of ideas to
center stage, but, crucially, it also argued that central to the War on Terror
is the formation of alliances between the U.S. and moderate, mainstream

voices within Islam. Given the threat posed by those who seek to "exploit Islam," "the strategy . . . is to empower the very people the terrorists most want to exploit: the faithful followers of Islam. We will continue to support political reforms that empower peaceful Muslims to practice and interpret their faith." In contrast to Britain and France, whose engagement with religious actors will take place mostly at the domestic level of analysis, the U.S. plans to support, encourage, and protect moderate Islam abroad. Around the world, the U.S. will engage "responsible Islamic leaders . . . to denounce an ideology that distorts and exploits Islam for destructive ends and defiles a proud religion" (USNSS 2006). "The most vital work will be done within the Islamic world itself," the report claims. As I show in chapter 5, this will include such countries as the Philippines, Indonesia, Jordan, and Afghanistan.

Bush's public speeches reflected this sudden turn to religion and a global war of ideas. In his 2006 State of the Union address Bush had spoken of "the perversion by a few of a noble faith into an ideology of terror." But a much more dramatic shift was evident in an August 2006 speech to the American Legion National Convention with the arresting title: "The Ideological Struggle of the 21st Century" (Bush 2006a). Nothing like it—or even the title—had been delivered by Bush before. Here Bush speaks in much more detail about Islam, claiming that "the enemies of liberty . . . take inspiration from different sources. Some are radicalized followers of the Sunni tradition . . . others are radicalized followers of the Shia tradition . . . still others are 'homegrown' terrorists" and "the link that spans sectarian divisions . . . is the rigid conviction that free societies are a threat to their twisted view of Islam" (Bush 2006a). As Tony Blair will do somewhat later, Bush proposes that current conflicts are manifestations of this deeper ideological war: "the battle for Iraq is now central to the ideological struggle of the 21st century" (Bush 2006a). Indeed, according to Bush, "the war we fight today is more than a military conflict; it is the decisive ideological struggle of the 21st century" (Bush 2006a). Finally, reflecting the call of the 2006 National Security Strategy for a new system of alliances with moderate Muslim reformers, the new ideological struggle of the 21st century requires "a bold new agenda to defeat the ideology of the enemy . . . we will take the side of democratic leaders and reformers across the Middle East" and will "support the voices of tolerance and moderation in the Muslim world" (Bush 2006a).

A few days later, on September 5, at the Hilton Hotel in Washington, D.C., Bush delivered a speech called "Remarks on the Global War on Terror: The Enemy in Their Own Words." Speaking to the Military Officers Association Bush introduced the audience to the new national security frame-work, stressing the formation of ideological alliance building abroad: "we're defeating the terrorists on the battlefield, and defeating their hateful ideol-ogy in the battle of ideas . . . we're taking the side of democratic leaders and moderates and reformers across the Middle East" (Bush 2006b). Bush then explicitly links this new strategy to U.S. national security: "we fight for this day, because the security of our own citizens depends on it. This is the great ideological struggle of the 21st century . . . all civilized nations are bound together in this struggle between moderation and extremism. By coming together, we will roll back this grave threat to our way of life" (Bush 2006b). Even secular Western states must take sides in the new, global war of ideas.

This new framing marked Bush's discourse on religion for the remainder of his presidency. Bush will repeat it in his address to the nation on the fifth anniversary of 9/11 on September 11, 2006, in his September 19 address to the UN General Assembly, his address to the nation about Iraq in 2007, his 2007 address in Prague, and his State of the Union addresses in 2007 and 2008. Throughout, Bush underscores the importance of forming alliances with acceptable Muslim voices to help fight and win the global war of ideas. In his 2007 address about Iraq, for example, Bush claims that "this war is more than a clash of arms; it is a decisive ideological struggle . . . so we ad-vance our own security interests by helping moderates and reformers and brave voices for democracy" (Bush 2007). Such a strategy will underpin the administrations' attempts to understand, engage, and influence the trajec-tory of Islam around the world.

"PSEUDO" RELIGION VS. "REAL" RELIGION: ISLAM IN BRITISH SECURITY DISCOURSE

On a 2006 U.S. tour, just as the U.S. was preparing to release its own Na-tional Security Strategy, British Prime Minister Tony Blair delivered a speech on the Middle East to the Los Angeles World Affairs Council in which he argued that there is in fact no "clash of civilizations" between the West and Islam. Rather, the notion of a clash of civilizations is the preserve of the "reactionary" mind. In the case of Al Qaeda, for example, the notion of a clash of civilizations served and continues to serve that organization tacti-cally. Blair argued that it had become clear to Al Qaeda by the late 1990s that the group could not frame its struggle as an inter-Islamic one because in doing so "they ran the risk that fellow Muslims—being as decent and fair-minded as anyone else—would choose to reject their fanaticism. A battle about Islam was just Muslim versus Muslim. They realised they had to create a completely different battle in Muslim minds: Muslim versus Western" (Blair 2006). While it began life as a potential future scenario by a Western academic, the clash of civilizations hypothesis quickly came to serve as a deliberate, strategic construction of fanatical Muslim minds. But the fanatics are mistaken, Blair argues, because the real clash lies not between Islam and the West, but rather in a "war" or "battle" within Islam itself between "moderate, mainstream" and "reactionary" forces (Blair 2006). Furthermore, the "war" within Islam requires that the West take sides, for the global contest impacts the security and safety of all "civilized" nations, especially Western liberal democracies.

The "war" within Islam impacts the security of Western liberal democracies in some unforeseen ways. Blair argues, in fact, that Islam's internal war underpins almost all of the well-known conflicts occurring on the contemporary geopolitical landscape: "in Lebanon, in Gaza, in Iraq, and add to that in Afghanistan, in Kashmir, in a host of other nations including now some in Africa—it is a global fight about global values; it is about modernisation, within Islam and outside of it" (Blair 2006). Furthermore, the conflict within Palestine between Hamas and Fatah is also a manifestation of this "battle within Islam" and "even the issue of Israel is just part of the same, wider struggle for the soul of the region." Nor is the battle within Islam limited to the conflicts in the Middle East: "the result of this struggle had effects wider than the region itself . . . plainly that applies to our own security . . . the read-across, for example, from the region to the Muslim communities in Europe is almost instant" (Blair 2006).

Expanding the scope even further, Blair links the "battle within Islam" to interstate alliances, globalization, and free trade. As Blair argues, a victory for the forces of moderate, mainstream Islam means a victory for global, neoliberal political economy.

> But there is a less obvious sense in which the outcome determines the success of our wider world-view. For me, a victory for the moderates means an Islam that is open: open to globalisation, open to working with others of different faiths, open to alliances with other nations . . . this struggle is in fact part of a far wider debate . . . the increasing divide today is between open and closed. Is the answer to globalisation, protectionism or free trade . . . is the answer to global security threats, isolationism or engagement? (Blair 2006)

Finally, Blair links interreligious conflict in Islam to the geopolitical landscape of the future. Islam's internal, spiritual war will impact the world's future balance of power.

> Think ahead. Think China, within 20 or 30 years, surely the world's other super-power. Think Russia and its precious energy reserves. Think India. I believe all of these great emerging powers want a benign relationship with the West. But I also believe that the stronger and more appealing our world-view is, the more it is seen as based not just on power but on justice, the easier it will be for us to shape the future in which Europe and the US will no longer, economically or politically, be transcendant. Long before then, we want Moderate, Mainstream Islam to triumph over Reactionary Islam." (Blair 2006)

Summing up the situation, Blair argues that the war or battle within Islam "is becoming itself a kind of surrogate for all the other issues the rest of the world has with the West. In other words, fail on this and across the range, everything gets harder" (Blair 2006). For Blair, then, there is no clash of civilizations between the West and Islam. Such us-versus-them thinking is the mark of reactionary, fanatical Muslim thought. Rather, at the global level, reactionary Islam poses a security threat not only to day-to-day civilian life, but to a host of other referent objects, including the peaceful outcome of a number of regional conflicts, the stability of Europe, the survival of the neoliberal political and economic order, and the ability of the West to "shape the future." Given all of this, what are Western states to do? The first step, according to Blair, is to "recognise this struggle for what it truly is"—a fundamentally religious struggle—for then "we would be at least along . . . the path to winning it" (Blair 2006). But how to fight and win a spiritual conflict that is at once local, national, regional, and global?

The unconventional nature of this war of ideas and values therefore requires "a complete renaissance of our strategy to defeat those that threaten us" (Blair 2006). Winning the war of ideas within Islam requires first that Western states to step outside of traditional security policy in order to strengthen the values that they share in common. Traditional security policy—military force, for example—will no longer do, because "Islamist extremism's whole strategy is based on a presumed sense of grievance that can motivate people to divide against each other. Our answer has to be a set of values strong enough to unite people with each other" (Blair 2006). At the center of this strategy will be a state-led attempt to take a side in this struggle for the soul of the world and "commit ourselves to . . . supporting Moderate, Mainstream Islam" (Blair 2006). This is an Islam—a moderate Islam—that represents the religion's "true voice," its "true essence," and its "moderate and true authority" (Blair 2007).

In a 2009 speech to the Chicago Council on Global Affairs, Blair goes into great detail about what distinguishes moderate from extremist or radical Islam. Here Blair reinforces the contrast between reactionary Islam as mere *ideology*, and moderate Islam as the true and authentic Islam (Blair 2009). Of what does the "true essence" of Islam consist? Tracing the roots of the tension to the late 19th and early 20th centuries, Blair argues that "the *authentic basis* of Islam, as laid down in the Qur'an, is progressive, humanitarian, sees knowledge and scientific advance as a duty, which is why for centuries Islam was the fount of so much invention and innovation" (Blair 2009). In contrast, like all mere ideologies, reactionary Islam is an instrumental position that can be changed, because it is not based on an enduring or genuine concern for justice, democracy, equality, or freedom; rather, radical ideologists "will espouse, tactically, any of these values if necessary" (Blair 2009). Moderate, mainstream Islam is open, loyal, authentic, and genuine; it expresses the "true essence" of that religion, the religion as it really is, and represents what it really means.

For Blair, the state is to play a leading role in achieving victory in the war over Islam's essence. To encourage and protect Islam's "authentic voice" and "the true essence of religious belief," the state must work closely with civil society (Blair 2007). Such work will be conducted on difficult, unfamiliar terrain for the liberal, secular state. The work may well be theological in nature. As Blair expressed it in more security-laden language, "extremism is *cloaked in religion*. . . so part of *defeating it lies also in religion*" (Blair 2009, emphasis mine). To the extent that it is, the hand of the state must remain hidden. The most effective and legitimate approach requires the formation of alliances within Muslim communities in Britain. As Blair argued, "ultimately, this battle can only be won within Islam itself and . . . across Islam today, we have allies . . . We need to support these allies. We need to work with them to allow their voice to be heard and their authenticity to be established" (Blair 2009). As Blair emphasized, "we have to be partners and helpers to the process of change and modernisation within Islam. We cannot do it. But we can support the doing of it by others" (Blair 2009).

Britain's engagement with religious actors focused on the domestic level of analysis. Consider the 2008 National Security Strategy of the United Kingdom. Reflecting the document's post–Cold War, widened conception of security, the threat of "violent extremists claiming to act in the name of Islam" is "a threat to all our communities, and an attack on our values and our way of life" (UKNSS 2008, 10). To challenge such "ideologies" the state will form alliances with civil society groups to "disrupt those who promote violent extremism and to support communities and institutions (for examples, mosques, colleges, universities, and prisons) in developing strategies to resist it" (26). These goals—challenging radical ideologies, supporting majority voices deemed peaceful—all require the "active participation of the widest cross-section of society, including central government, voluntary and community groups, regional and local government . . . it means ensuring that we empower local authorities, institutions and communities to deliver local solutions to local issues" (26). The 2008 National Security Strategy of the United Kingdom thus articulates the underlying approach to security that will justify state involvement at home to promote moderate, authentic, and true Islam.

In addition, the strategy for promoting moderate Islam also expanded to other departments in the British government. As Britain's "Preventing Violent Extremism" report argued, the state must expand the range of securitizing actors beyond traditional confines to include "departments and agencies who would not traditionally be involved in national security" (PVE 2008, 13). To achieve this, the British government must build an understanding with its key Muslim partners of "*the national strategic framework and their part in delivering it*" (26, emphasis mine; see also PET 2005, 75). Foremost among these are religious intellectuals, imams, and theologians from Britain's Muslim communities. These state-supported religious interlocutors will be expected to share the responsibility for creating and disseminating an authentic, true, and moderate Islam. The issue becomes, then, whether Muslim communities will accept their new role as securitizing actors in the UK's national security strategy.

MACROSECURITIZATION OF RELIGION: FRANCE

Nicolas Sarkozy's public discourse on Islam and religion paralleled that of Bush and Blair in many ways. Like Bush and Blair, we find Sarkozy disavowing the notion of a clash of civilizations and replacing it with a "debate" or "struggle" within Islam between "the forces of moderation" and the "most conservative" versions of the religion. Like Blair, Sarkozy's discourse about religion and security translated into policy at the domestic level of analysis, where Sarkozy proposed the formation of alliances between the French state and Muslim civil society groups in order to develop a moderate version of Islam to protect it from the forces of ideological distortion.

The first discursive step Sarkozy makes is to deny, as Bush and Blair do, that there is a clash of civilizations between the West and Islam, and replace this with a struggle *within* Islam that underpins other conflicts across the globe. As early as 2003, when he served as France's interior minister, Sarkozy had claimed that the tension between moderate and conservative Islam is a worldwide feature of that religion: "this debate between the most moderate and most conservative forces is going on in Egypt and elsewhere" and so "our choice . . . is to pursue the dialogue between religions which is absolutely necessary if we are to understand each other and prevent clashes between civilizations, and to do so with the most moderate forces" (Sarkozy 2003b). Later, as president, Sarkozy remarked in a 2007 speech to the Opening Conference of Ambassadors that there are three main challenges facing the world, and the first and most important is "how to prevent a confrontation between Islam and the West," a confrontation called for by "extremist groups such as al-Qaeda that dream of establishing a caliphate from Indonesia to Nigeria, rejecting all openness, all modernity, every hint of diversity" (Sarkozy 2007a). Defeating the narrative of a clash of civilizations is thus a global effort.

Sarkozy connects a number of other geopolitical issues to the war of ideas, which on their face to have little to do with religion or to the "debate" within Islam. In a speech in Algeria, Sarkozy argues that defeating the clash of civilizations involves "helping—as France is proposing—the Muslim countries to gain access to the energy of the future, nuclear power" (Sarkozy 2007a). Later in the same speech he remarks that "I say on behalf of France that the sharing of civilian nuclear energy will be one of the foundations of the pact of trust that the West must move with the Muslim world" (2007b). What holds for Algeria also holds for the Mediterranean region as a whole. In Sarkozy's discourse the region has an important role to play in the global war of ideas. According to Sarkozy, the Mediterranean world is unique precisely because it does *not* conjure the image of a clash of civilizations or a new war of religion; this is why Sarkozy proposes his "Union of the Mediterranean," a deepening of the economic, military, and civilian ties between and among the European and North African powers that border the sea. Sarkozy considers this proposal for increased interdependence and mutual support as central to undermining the concept of the clash of civilizations between Islam and the West (Sarkozy 2007a; also 2007b). For the threat of a clash of civilizations is "not hypothetical" and can only be prevented by greater ideological, political, and economic ties between France, the European Union, and the Mediterranean region (Sarkozy 2007b). Thus the Mediterranean countries must take the leading role in ensuring victory for an "Islamic Enlightenment" against the "mortal threat" of "barbarism" (2007b; 2008b). If they do not, Sarkozy argued in Tunisia, then "the clash of civilizations and religions . . . will be unavoidable" (2008b). Finally, much as Blair linked victory in the war within Islam to the survival of the globalized liberal economic order, Sarkozy too links the development of a "humanistic and open Islam, an Islam of Enlightenment" to the expansion of the free market economy in Morocco, Algeria, Tunisia, Jordan, and Indonesia (Sarkozy 2007b).

Having laid out the proposition that the clash of civilizations is not a fait accompli, Sarkozy argues that it is France that has the most important role to play in preventing the clash between the West and Islam. As in Britain, the solution is for the state to encourage the development of moderate, mainstream Islam in the name of national and international security. What is needed, Sarkozy argued in 2007, is to "encourage and help the forces of moderation and modernity in each Muslim country to enable an open and tolerant Islam—an Islam that accepts diversity as an enrichment—to prevail . . . I call on our cooperation to strengthen programs focused on openness and dialogue among societies, in conjunction—why not—with representatives of Islam in France" (Sarkozy 2007a).

As in the cases of Bush and Blair, Sarkozy's public discourse on religion and Islam is reflected in the country's wider thinking about national and international security. Particularly with regards to the domestic level of analysis, French discourse and strategy on Islam is similar to Britain's. In 2006, for example, a security working group under the direction of French Prime Minister Villepin produced the White Paper on Terrorism and Security in France (*La France face au Terrorisme*). In this document, religion and religious ideas—especially interpretations of Islam—are framed as important security matters for the state: "France . . . is undertaking substantive action whose success requires it to maintain constant vigilance . . . and win the battle of ideas" (*La France Face a Terrorisme* 2006, 97). As in Britain, winning the "battle of ideas" requires expanding the security agenda beyond traditional confines, for "this . . . cannot be left solely to the specialized counter-terrorism security agencies. This new dimension of the 'esprit de défense' must be widely promoted and shared throughout French society" (98). Winning the global war of ideas is not simply a matter of combatting terrorism but signifies a much larger struggle in which the Western state must cultivate alliances to help tip the balance in its favor. What is needed is a concentrated engagement by the state at the domestic level of analysis to cultivate such alliances, especially with Muslim representative organizations.

Like Blair, Sarkozy is conscious of the fact that something must be done to encourage and protect moderate and modern interpretations of Islam and that doing so successfully is a matter of national security. Yet the two men faced a common problem: secular states must tread lightly in this territory. Both therefore take great pains to reiterate the distinction between matters of theology and matters of politics. Sarkozy is aware that France's national tradition of secularity or *laicite* is a double-edged sword: while *laicite* represents a path to integration and security for France's Muslim communities, the principle itself may also prevent the state from taking measures to develop the necessary interpretations of Islam in order to foster such integration. In his 2003 speech after discussing the formation of Muslim representative organizations in France, Sarkozy hastens to address an issue that must surely have been on the audience's mind: "there is no question of making it (Islam) uniform . . . there is no question of singling out and distinguishing one official form of Islam. *It is not for the Republic to act as the arbiter of your internal debates. These religious, internal debates are not its affair*" (Sarkozy 2003b; emphasis mine). As the following chapters show, the distinction between theology and politics will prove very difficult to maintain as the state moves to form alliances and partnerships with Muslim representative organizations in order to develop and protect moderate interpretations of Islam.

CONCLUSION: FROM "CLASH" TO RELIGIOUS ENGAGEMENT

As this chapter demonstrates, George W. Bush, Tony Blair, and Nicolas Sarkozy faced the difficult dilemma of how to describe the "enemy"—the existential security threat—in the War on Terror. There seemed to be an "irreducibly religious" dimension to the conflict, yet the War on Terror could not be framed in exclusively religious terms. Doing so would only fuel the argument that Western political elites sought to foster a clash of civilizations between Islam and the West. A state discourse approaching anywhere near the concept of a clash of civilizations would play directly into the hands of Al Qaeda's leadership, it was thought, and if one examines bin Laden and Zawahiri's writings from the post–9/11 period, there is some truth in this concern. Defeating the notion of a clash of civilizations between Islam and the West became especially important for Bush and Blair, for neither could afford to have the allied invasions of Afghanistan and Iraq interpreted as a war or attack on Muslims or the religion of Islam. And with a steady stream of news stories about desecrations of the Koran, Bible verses inscribed on U.S. guns, and the use of torture techniques deliberately designed to play on detainee's cultural and religious taboos, it is little wonder that Bush, having himself once slipped in describing the U.S.-led War on Terror as a crusade, took every opportunity to stress that the War on Terror was not a War on Islam. Whatever the underlying motivations may have been, all three leaders exerted much effort to short-circuit the clash of civilizations narrative and find another way of describing the security situation they faced.

In public speeches and national security strategies, a new discourse emerged to replace the clash of civilizations. According to the new discursive frame, the religion of Islam emerges as divided against itself between moderate and radical camps, with the former synonymous with what Islam "really is" or "really means" and the latter populated by those seeking to distort or pervert Islam's true message for political, ideological ends. Underpinning this discourse of moderate versus extremist interpretations of Islam lay a more general distinction about religion itself. Religion has an *essence* that is authentic and true: an essence that is liberal, democratic, and tolerant. It is not terrorist violence that threatens the existence of this new civil religion, for violence can never drain the true faith or the universal appeal of its theopolitical core. Rather, what threatens this post–9/11 political theology is ideology—the twisting of religion for radical political ends.

A new civil religion—a *global* civil religion—thus appears in post–9/11 state discourse as a *referent object* for security. Much depends on the survival of this referent object, for it is the true, authentic religious faith that forms the core of Western civilization and its political values. Because the stakes are so high and the global war within Islam lies beneath the surface of conflicts all around the world, the West—and especially the Western, secular state—must take sides in this war. The state must form alliances with those Muslim voices who express the real, true essence of Islam, a nonpolitical, *spiritual* essence that overlaps with Western political virtues.

It is possible to arrange this post–9/11 security discourse in a more systematic fashion. All three discourses have a macro-structure in common (see table 1). The U.S., Britain, and France would each build off of this common discursive approach to support the development of the new civil religion at different levels of analysis. Thus this macro-level securitization of religion has different variations at each level (see table 2).

In this new war of ideas, victory lies not in military operations or the clash of arms but rather in the *discursive* field, in the defeat of the narrative of the clash of civilizations and its replacement with an Islam that is compatible both with Western values in general, and with specific, national values at the domestic level. This requires the Western state to expand its range of securitizing actors. Alliances must be formed with reliable Muslim interlocutors who will develop, protect, and promulgate the message that an enlightened, moderate, and modern Islam is compatible with community cohesion in a multicultural, multifaith society (Britain), the principles of *laicite* and republican citizenship (France), and the values of democracy and freedom (United States).

As the following empirical chapters of this book show, the general discursive framework that all three states shared translated into similar policies, such as incorporating references to religion and Islam in counterterrorism and deradicalization programs, training police and security forces in what Islam really means, promoting targeted outreach to Muslim communities, (re)training religious leaders in secular, liberal values, and most importantly, establishing or cultivating relationships with "reliable" Muslim representative organizations (see, for example, Bowen 2004; Caeiro 2005; Haddad and Golson 2007). All three states enacted programs to encourage the development of Islam's authentic voices and promote the emergence of a global civil

TABLE 1.   Securitization of Religion: General Discursive Structure

	Threat	**Referent Object**
Macro Framework:	Religion as ideology	Religion as "true faith"
U.S., Britain, France	False interpretations of Islam	Islam's true meaning
	Radical Islam	Moderate Islam
	Totalitarian values	Liberal Political Values
	Perversions of religion →	(Inter)national Security

TABLE 2.   Discursive Structure by Levels of Analysis

	Threat	**Referent Object**	**Solution?**
International:			
U.S.	Radical Islam	Moderate Islam = *Democracy, Freedom*	Alliances abroad (Smart Power)
Domestic:			
Britain	Radical Islam	Moderate Islam = *British-Muslim identity*	Alliances at home (Community Cohesion)
France	Radical Islam	Moderate Islam = *"Islam of France"*	Alliances at home (Positive *Laicite*)

religion more in line with secular liberal priorities. Britain, France, and the U.S. concentrated their efforts on encouraging religious reform in the name of national and international security by attempting to gain the support and allegiance of religious allies in delivering the security agenda.

Such policies are indeed out of the ordinary for three Western states that maintain that secularism, whether Judeo-Christian or *laicist*, is at the core of their national identity (Hurd 2007). Blair and Sarkozy especially were keenly aware that the formation or expansion of alliances with religious organizations at the domestic level of analysis for purposes of national security would take the state into unfamiliar terrain, and both took great pains to justify their policies and reassure the multiple relevant audiences that the secular state had no interest in intervening in theological matters. This reflects the general problem that Western secular states face in the post–9/11 world, a world in which states can no longer ignore but must acknowledge and engage with religious actors and ideas. The more religion finds its way onto widening security agendas, however, the more treacherous the terrain becomes. This is precisely why in the previous chapter I argued that it is crucial to consider religion a fluid category in international affairs. For in selecting religious allies, discussing religious ideas, and promoting religious reform for national security, it is unavoidable that the state will at some point need to draw a distinction between what can properly be considered religious and what cannot.

Thus Bush, Blair, and Sarkozy point out that they have no intention of intervening in religious matters. The project is rather to express arm's length support for certain interpretations of Islam. Although their aims are similar, the fortunes of the U.S, Britain, and France differ markedly in this regard. As table 2 shows, there is a difference between the referent object for security at the international and domestic levels of analysis. At the domestic level of analysis religion as a referent object is linked more closely to national identity and loyalty to the state and its core values. In Britain and France, the project of developing moderate interpretations of Islam is one over which British and French Muslim communities must take ownership. According to Blair and Sarkozy, this is part of these communities' civic and political obligation. The problem with this domestic-level securitization of religion and Islam, and the possible reason for its failure, is that one's status as a threat, and therefore one's acceptance by the national community, is made contingent upon a particular interpretation of one's religion. Indeed, as the following two chapters show, both Britain and France attempted to enact the combination of religion and security into concrete policy. Both states expected official Muslim representative organizations to do the job of promulgating the message, which not only did little to assuage the perception of state meddling in religious matters but exacerbated anxieties by linking collective identity to questions of loyalty, security, and political obligation. These proved to be toxic combinations that in both cases led to a failed securitization of religion.

3 ✦ Britain

Religion as a Weapon

No point in being "squeamish," proclaimed Hazel Blears, Britain's former Secretary of State for Communities and Local Government. The evidence was in. According to a 2009 BBC poll, more than three in five Britons believed that "national laws should be influenced by traditional religious values" and that "faith should have a bigger role in the public sphere" (Blears 2009). Such findings helped reinforce what New Labour had been arguing all along: that religion and religious organizations were an integral part of safe, cohesive communities, and so religion should play a more visible role in public life. Civil society organizations such as the Muslim Council of Britain agreed, arguing that "religious faith has the potential to promote British society's cohesion and regeneration" (Muslim Council of Britain 2002, 2–3).

Britain's think-tank community echoed the new approach. One prominent pro-New Labour think tank called Demos argued that the country's "government and security forces" need to "get a grip on faith" (Briggs, Fieschi, and Lownsbrough, 61). According to Demos, police officials, local government authorities, and ordinary citizens must, in the name of community cohesion and national security, root their work in an "understanding of faith, without which it is easy for government and security forces to misread the signs within the community" (15). Understanding "faith" thus requires distinguishing between which religious practices should be considered normal and unthreatening and which should not. In 2008, the Religion and Society section of the UK's Arts and Humanities Research Council reiterated that "religious knowledge is essential in fighting violent ideology" (Arts and

Humanities 2008, 16). Other organizations such as the Quilliam Foundation, "the world's first counter-extremist think-tank," expressed similar sentiments (Quilliam Foundation).

If religion played a central role in creating secure and cohesive British communities, it stood to reason that religion could also help to counter "violent extremism." Tony Blair set the tone in this regard when he remarked in a 2009 speech that part of defeating "ideology cloaked in religion lies also in religion . . . in a consistent and clear critique of religious error by religious leaders," especially by Britain's Muslim communities (Blair 2009). Seen from this perspective there is a clear subtext to Blears's admonition against collective British squeamishness and "creeping oversensitivity" about the role of religion in public life: do not fear if the state takes steps to increase its engagement with religious actors, for a public mandate exists for such intervention. Echoing Blair, Blears went on to argue that "far from being part of the problem, faith can be part of the solution . . . it is often those people with the weakest understanding of faith who are the most susceptible to extremist messages" (Blears 2009). As these quotations suggest, religious faith must be strengthened for reasons of national security. This notion, that religious faith is a vital ingredient of British national security, lies at the core of Britain's "Prevent" program for combating violent extremism under the heading "Building Faith Capacity." Following 9/11, the British state took a leading role in building the nation's "faith capacity" by promoting, encouraging, and even funding the activity of a variety of religious actors.

Britain's incorporation of religion into national security policy reflected a widened approach to national security following 9/11. The attacks of September 11, 2001, made clear to the British government the need to rethink traditional conceptions of security. The Blair government recognized that traditional means such as counterterrorism legislation, tighter immigration policies, and increased intelligence collection and policing were necessary but not sufficient to deal with the many dimensions of the threat the country faced. Foremost among these, as the previous chapter demonstrated, was the war of ideas taking place within the religion of Islam. In a new security context in which pseudo-religious ideas posed an existential threat to real religion and the real authentic meaning of Islam, a new approach was needed.

To meet this new form of threat, the Blair government launched its CONTEST strategy, a wide-ranging program of domestic counterterrorism. CONTEST had four strands: Pursue, Prevent, Protect, and Prepare. While the Pursue, Protect, and Prepare elements of the program focused on more traditional aspects of security policy such as policing, domestic legislation, intelligence-gathering, and securing the country's infrastructure, the Prevent strand was unique, dealing instead with those individuals who "reject and undermine our shared values and jeopardize community cohesion" (HC 65 2010, 5). In other words, to protect national security, the British government would have to take a step into the realm of ideas. Some employed in traditional domestic security sectors found this odd. As one British policeman put it, "we do law enforcement . . . but what we are being expected to do is something that is slightly strange . . . which is prevention of ideas . . ." (HC 65 2010, 19).

In the context of New Labour, involvement in the realm of ideas meant involvement in matters of religion. In its early iterations, the purpose of the Prevent program was to foster a mainstream, moderate version of Islam in the name of national security. In July 2005 the Home Office had convened a number of working groups on various topics under the heading of "Preventing Extremism Together" (PET 2005). In the reports from those working groups, the link between religion and national security comes clearly into focus. According to the report, "a pseudo-religious imperative" threatens the security of UK communities, and "this is an ideological arena that can only be responded to and corrected by theological confutation and intra-Muslim engagement (PET 2005, 94). Given that the threat the nation faces is ideological—*pseudo religious*—the most important goal of the Prevent strategy is to enhance "the role of the Muslim community in the promotion of national security" (75). Doing so meant encouraging the construction of moderate Islam; the report goes on to argue "the solution to challenging radical 'pseudo-religious' interpretations is not 'less Islam': it is through disseminating a more authentic understanding of Islam" (91).

The Prevent strategy reflected New Labour's vision that the most effective way to build secure, cohesive communities was to direct state efforts toward those communities deemed most vulnerable to ideological or pseudo-religious intrusion, and to do this by supporting moderate, more authentic understandings of the religion of Islam. Under the Prevent program, the British state would play a leading role in engaging religious actors to encourage, develop, protect, and disseminate Islam's moderate voices. Indeed, following the London bombings of July 7, 2005, the Blair government elevated the Prevent strategy to an independent policy initiative (Thomas 2010, 443). Moreover, because the strategy of challenging pseudo-religious interpretations of religion with "mainstream" or "more authentic" interpretations was so closely intertwined with fostering New Labour's vision of community cohesion, the government moved responsibility for the Prevent program from the Home Office to the newly created Department for Communities and Local Government. In April 2007, the department released an in-depth strategy for tackling violent extremism, strengthening religious faith, and promoting moderate Islam called "Preventing Violent Extremism—Winning Hearts and Minds."

The Prevent program was further refined throughout 2007, 2008, and 2009. A pressing task in these years was figuring out how to frame the program and sell it to the public. As Jonathan Evans, then head of the MI5 put it, close attention must be paid to "our use of language . . . we are tackling a threat which finds its roots in ideology, so words really do matter" (Norton-Taylor 2007). In 2007, a Home Office reshuffle led to the creation of a new Research, Communication, and Information Unit (RCIU) specifically tasked to draw up and disseminate "counter-narratives" and support "alternative voices" in the Muslim community (Norton-Taylor 2007). A significant part of the RCIU's job was to rethink the discourse used. A 2007 cable from the U.S. embassy, London reported for example that the newly created RCIU was debating "the advantage of using the word 'mainstream' to define common values as opposed to 'the West' which can have negative connotations" (Tuttle 2007a). Here we can see the creation of the British government's public framing of the PREVENT strategy. According to the state, the leaders of local Muslim community organizations—"mainstream Muslim voices"—are best placed to protect Britain's "shared values" from "perverted forms of Islam" (Smith 2008a).

The state understood very well that it was locked into a war of words, ideas, and images with a pseudo-religious enemy. To win the war, the counterstrategy would also need to be discursive. In 2008 Home Secretary Jacqui Smith delivered a speech on the Prevent strategy to the Smith Institute in London (Smith 2008a) in which she argued that

> It is important . . . that we use the right language . . . It's not semantics or political correctness to describe Al Qaeda as 'anti-Islamic'. It's the truth . . . it reflects the impact that the language and phrases we use can have, on our communities and on a wider audience. Violent extremists are themselves very careful with their words . . . manipulating theology as well as history and contemporary politics.

Smith here underscores that the language used to describe the threat that Britain faces is not simply a matter of "semantics" but impacts the way in which the government's Prevent program will be received by Britain's communities. As Smith implies, it is probably true that describing Al Qaeda in the reverse way—as "Islamic"—would give offense to many British Muslims. Smith reminds the audience however that the act of description is not simply an exercise in political correctness. By immediately making reference to "violent extremists" and *their* use of words, the passage also implies that Britain's Prevent strategy must itself include a discursive component, because the conflict between Britain and its "anti-Islamic" adversaries is itself partly a conflict over representation and framing.

In a meeting with Smith in London the previous year, former U.S. Homeland Security Secretary Michael Chertoff asked her how the UK government described the "radicalized." Smith replied that "criminals" and "murderers" were often used, "but if the Islamic context is removed, something is missing" (Tuttle 2007b). As we have seen, in the case of the U.S., too, those who helped draft the 2006 National Security Strategy felt that there was an irreducibly religious element to the threat the nation faced that must be described. It is indeed important to refer to the religious context, Smith now argued, given that the ultimate goal is "to enlist the Muslim community against its fringes" (Tuttle 2007b).

Thus the Prevent program is based on a deliberate discursive strategy calculated to develop a moderate form of the religion of Islam. How things are described not only has concrete effects on British communities, but if the threat to be faced is based on miscategorization, manipulation, false theological interpretations, and pseudo religion, the threat must be countered on its own terms. If religion is used as a weapon by the enemy, the state would fight back with religion too. The new state-led theostrategy must pit the truth—what Islam really means—against pseudo religion. As Jacqui Smith remarked, the true existential threat to Britain lies in *religion as ideology*, a "detailed ideology that draws on the language of" and operates "in the guise of" religion (Smith 2008b; see also Smith 2008c).

At the center of the new theostrategic approach lay the notion of "building faith capacity."

> We are clear that it is not the role of Government to seek to change any religion or religious community. Interpretations of the religion within any faith community are entirely a matter for itself. However, where Islamic theology is being used to justify violent extremist rhetoric or activity, to the extent that national security is under threat, Government will answer calls to assist communities to *reinforce faith*

understanding and thereby build resilience to extremist interpretations of Islam. (Preventing Violent Extremism 2008, 38; emphasis mine)

To "reinforce faith understanding" the British government elected to fund a number of concrete initiatives. These included setting up what Blears described as a "theology board" of Muslim academics, theologians, and community representatives in order to "lead thinking on Islam in a modern context" and raise awareness of the "real, peaceful Islam" practiced by the majority of British Muslims (Blears 2008). This initiative led to the formation of a group of Muslim scholars and community leaders at Cambridge University. According to one news report, "the board's work will focus on examining issues related to Islam's place in Britain and obligations as a citizen" (Casciani 2008). The theology board initiative thus linked together the issues of theology and religious faith to the question of loyalty and political obligation.

A second initiative involved the training—or, in some cases, retraining—of imams. To achieve the diffusion of moderate or mainstream Islam and also promote community cohesion, the government cosponsored with the Muslim Council of Britain the creation of a group known as the Mosques and Imams National Advisory Board (MINAB). The board was tasked with establishing "a framework of minimum requirements for all imams engaged by the state" (Preventing Violent Extremism 2007, 11). Such a body was to play a key role in supporting "mainstream interpretations of the role of Islam in modern societies" against those who seek to exploit a "lack of understanding" of the religion (Preventing Violent Extremism 2007, 5). As Blears put it, responsible leadership includes "delivering enhanced standards for our mosques and religious leaders—and that must include, for example, ensuring appropriate monitoring of what is preached in our mosques and the literature and other material distributed in our religious institutions" (Blears 2007). Some Muslim organizations quickly took to the initiative. Britain's Bradford Council of Mosques for example developed teaching materials and curricula designed to "demonstrate clearly how Islamic values are entirely consistent with core British values" (Preventing Violent Extremism 2007, 5). As the 2005 document "Preventing Extremism Together" put it, the UK government seeks to "promote/develop . . . a Muslim leadership appropriate for 21st century multi-cultural Britain—this means a leadership not just in terms of a skills set but a leadership capable of rethinking the universal principles and values of Islam for today's Britain" (2005, 8).

Other initiatives included expanding the state's relationship with Muslim representative organizations such as the Muslim Council of Britain (MCB) and forming new ones such as the Sufi Muslim Council. Launched in 2006 by Ruth Kelly, Secretary of State for Communities and Local Government, the Sufi Muslim Council was created to represent and promote moderate Muslim voices to help fight extremism, and received over 200,000 pounds to do so (Thomas 2010, 447). Other groups created to help articulate and encourage the spread of moderate Islam include the Radical Middle Way, the Quilliam Foundation, and the British Muslim Forum, all of which received considerable amounts from the UK government (for the amounts see Thomas 2010).

As the British state reached out to expand the range of nonstate actors to help execute the new security strategy on the ground, it also began to expand the number of securitizing actors within the state as well. By 2008 the British Government's security strategy "has increased in scope . . . involving departments and agencies who would not traditionally be involved in national security" such as the Department of Communities and Local Government and the Ministry of Education (Preventing Violent Extremism 2008, 13). In an example of how the securitization of religion reached into Britain's system of higher education, former Higher Education Minister Bill Rammell announced in 2007 that Islamic Studies would henceforth be considered a "strategically important subject" in British higher education (Department of Children, Schools, and Families 2007). According to the website of the ministry, "Islamic studies is to be designated 'strategically' important because of its contribution to the UK's political and cultural capital . . . this would in turn contribute to preventing violent extremism in the name of Islam and improving community cohesion" (Department of Children, Schools, and Families 2007).

Such expansions of the security sector and the number of securitizing actors raised the government's expectations and increased the responsibilities of Britain's Muslim communities. Blears claimed that British Muslims and Muslim organizations must demonstrate "responsible leadership," which involves "supporting the police and security services in their efforts to tackle terrorism so that all in society can be safe and secure" (Blears 2007). In the case of the MINAB, the government pledged to "continue to work with the MINAB to ensure they are capable of stepping up to the challenge of their role as the national body with responsibility for mosques and imams" (Preventing Violent Extremism 2007, 12). Through imam training, theology boards, traveling road shows,[1] and the formation of Muslim representative organizations, the British government thus sought to build an understanding among key Muslim partners of "the national strategic framework and their part in delivering it" (Preventing Violent Extremism 2008, 26).

As early as 2006, tensions were already on the rise between the British government and the country's Muslim communities. In a confidential cable back to Washington, staff at the U.S. embassy, London reported that the British government's attempts to engage its Muslim communities were not going well (Tuttle 2006). Muslim reaction to a series of raids, arrests, frozen assets, and search procedures culminated in a public letter signed by Muslim MPs, Muslim members of the House of Lords, and some 38 Muslim organizations across Britain. The letter argued that British foreign policy, especially the country's participation in the invasion of Iraq and the Israel-Palestine situation, provided "ammunition to extremists" and put British lives at risk. According to the cable, the British government reacted in anger at the mere suggestion that British foreign policy was to blame, calling the idea "dreadful . . . a distorted view of the world, a distorted view of life . . . facile, dangerous, and foolish" (Tuttle 2006). Frustrated, British Communities Secretary Ruth Kelly and ministers from the Home Office ratcheted up the pressure on the country's Muslim communities, called on leading Muslim representative leaders to deliver the message that "Muslim leaders must do more to tackle extremism inside their community" (Tuttle 2006). In the following years, tensions continued to mount between Britain's Muslim communities and the British government. Disillusionment from both formal and informal Muslim organizations and communities would disturb and disorient the British government strategy at various crucial points between 2006 and 2010, and culminate when the new Conservative government of David Cameron completely reoriented the Prevent strategy away from community cohesion, and away from the securitization of religion.

Muslim Representative Organizations

As Britain's Prevent strategy continued to evolve between 2006 and 2010, the UK government worked closely with already existing Muslim representative organizations such as the Muslim Council of Britain (MCB) and, when necessary, created new ones, such as the Sufi Muslim Council (SMC) and the Quilliam Foundation. Underpinning these partnerships was the discourse of moderate Islam. Before long, however, it became clear to many that the government's interventionist approach had fatal flaws. While many of Britain's Muslim organizations realized that the Prevent program had good intentions, and thereby sought to improve, and not dismantle it, the way in which the program was framed—around a discourse of religion and security—created apprehension and mistrust among them.

Before I detail the objections of Muslim organizations to the Prevent program, it is first necessary to highlight the general profile of Muslim communities in Britain. When one talks about Muslim communities or British Muslims, one always risks overgeneralization. Muslim communities in Britain are not monolithic. The UK is home to about 2 million Muslims, about 3 percent of the UK's population (Muslim Council of Britain 2013). 74 percent of the UK's Muslim population are from an Asian ethnic background with the majority being Pakistani (43 percent) along with Bangladeshi (16 percent) followed by Indian (8 percent). The remainder of British Muslims (about 11 percent) are from a White ethnic background, including "white British origin" or Turkish, Cypriot, Arab, and Eastern European. Moreover, a substantial portion of the UK's Muslim population were not born in the UK: estimated figures are 39 percent born in Asia (Pakistan, 18 percent; Bangladesh, 9 percent; India, 3 percent) and 9 percent were born in Africa, mainly Somalia and Kenya. Another 4 percent of Britain's Muslim population were born in Europe, but outside of the UK, such as Turkey and the former Yugoslavia. Moreover, with 34 percent of Muslims under the age of 16 in 2001, Muslims have the youngest age profile of all Britain's religious groups: less than one in ten British Muslims were aged 65 or older.

One concrete example will help to illustrate the diversity of Britain's Muslim population, and the divergent interests and opinions that exist within it. On October 9, 2007, the United States' Special Representative for Muslim Outreach, Farah Pandith, travelled to East London for a series of events in order to hear the perspectives of Muslim youth. In the audience were students, journalists, local political leaders, representing a broad cross-section of opinion. An embassy cable reporting on the meeting noted that "the journalists kept interjecting foreign policy issues such as Iraq and Israel/Palestine" but "the young people stressed that while those issues might be of some concerns, the real issues in their lives are jobs, education, and empowerment" (Tuttle 2007a). Differences in perspective emerged within Muslim youth as well. The following day, at an event sponsored by the New Century

Foundation, a U.S. embassy official noticed a profound difference of opinion between those young people "in their mid-20s with graduate degrees" and "the group of more impoverished youth in East London." The former group "focused entirely on foreign policy, and more specifically on U.S. foreign policy . . . many of them had radical views, including that 'America had 9/11 coming to it.'" In contrast, the latter group focused more on "integration and opportunity issues inside of Britain" (Tuttle 2007a). Given the different profiles of these two groups of Muslim youths, such information may not be particularly surprising. Nonetheless, such differences highlight how difficult it is for any overarching Muslim representative group in Britain to faithfully represent the interests of the country's Muslim community, and especially when such organizations are charged with promoting, protecting, and encouraging a moderate or authentic version of Islam. Indeed, given such a multilayered, complex community with multiple lines of tension and fracture, what could *mainstream* or *authentic* Islam mean?

Given the diversity within the UK's Muslim communities, it is unsurprising that Muslim representative organizations in Britain reflect a wide swath of opinion and often struggle to speak with a unified voice. Perhaps the best-known Muslim representative organization in Britain is the Muslim Council of Britain (MCB). Founded in 1997, the MCB is an umbrella group that includes more than 500 affiliated Muslim organizations from across Britain and including Northern Ireland (Klausen 2005a, 34). The MCB was the UK government's preferred interlocutor with Britain's Muslim communities. The close relationship between the MCB and the British government culminated with the election of the Blair government, when, in the words of one scholar, "the MCB's consolidation of a 'new', professionalized and media-friendly Muslim representative body coincided with the election of New Labour" (McLaughlin 2006, 61). Indeed, the MCB's passionate arguments about the importance of religion in British public life comported well with New Labour's vision of a Britain in which religious faith was a key component of community cohesion in a multifaith, multiethnic, and multicultural country.

Yet the more the British government forced the connection between religion and national security, the rockier the relationship between the MCB and the British government became. Very soon after the bombings of July 7, 2005, the MCB harshly rebuked the Blair government, claiming that "you cannot assume that Muslims are collectively responsible for the actions of a few," said Inayat Bunglawa, MCB media spokesman (Tuttle 2006). In the wake of the 7/7 bombings, the official reaction of the MCB to the government's Prevent strategy was largely negative. While noting that "efforts to promote community cohesion are laudible," the organization argued that such initiatives will be "met with skepticism and mistrust," especially "in a country where the state is largely neutral on theological matters" (Muslim Council of Britain 2008).

Relations were also strained over the topic of imam training programs. The notion of training imams to preach more responsible versions of Islam and to prove their "British" credentials was inherently controversial. In 2005, opposition from Muslims, Hindus, and Sikhs forced the government to abandon a mandatory "Britishness test" for foreign-born imams (Shepherd 2007). In the wake of the 7/7 attacks, however, the government returned to the idea, seeking to include imam training into its Prevent program; imam training was elevated to an important part of Britain's security and counter-terrorism strategy. Shortly before stepping down as prime minister in 2007 Blair had delivered a speech in which he called on foreign-born imams in Britain to receive training in British language, society, and culture from British universities. According to a current newspaper report, driving the Blair government's concern over radical imams was the fact that over 600 of Britain's 1,350 mosques "are run by the Deobandi sect, which espouses a puritan version of Islam; many of the sect's seminaries for example outlaw art, music, television, and chess, demand full covering for women and consider football 'a cancer that has corrupted our youth'" (Norfolk 2007). While not all Deobandi members espouse violence, some do, and such statistics proved disturbing enough for the UK government to make imam training a high priority in the PREVENT strategy. One spokesman for the Department of Communities is reported to have said, "we have a detailed strategy to ensure imams properly represent . . . mainstream moderate opinion and promote shared values like tolerance and respect for the rule of law" (Norfolk 2007).

Complicating matters, however, was that fact that the Deobandi sect had substantial representation on the Muslim Council of Britain. Thus, from the point of the UK government, the MCB appeared best placed to run the imam training part of the Prevent initiative, and in 2007, the MINAB organization was formed under the auspices of the MCB, facilitated by the Department of Communities and Local Government and funded with Prevent money. To be sure, some members of the MCB welcomed the initiative. Sheikh Ibrahim Mogra, for example, defended the state-sponsored training of imams, arguing that the creation of the MINAB group had in fact been driven by Britain's Muslims rather than by the government (Ford 2008). But even Mogra's enthusiasm for the program came with a qualification: "anything that helps to make our communities stronger should be welcomed," he remarked, "provided that it's not used to isolate, control, or change what a community is . . . we've made it clear that it's not for government to touch our theology or touch the way we train our people" (Ford 2008).

The initiative was met with skepticism from other civil society groups as well. The National Muslim Women's Advisory Group, which had in fact been formed by the Department of Communities and Local Government in 2008, observed that "MINAB has failed to win confidence at grassroots level irrespective of their propaganda, too often, by the same old community leaders with vested political interests" (HC 65, ev. 169).

The issue of imam training in Britain illustrates well many of the important tensions that began to surface between the UK government and the country's Muslim organizations, and between and among those organizations themselves, especially after the 7/7 bombings when the New Labour government became ever more deeply involved in religion. Foremost among such tensions was the very idea—again, encapsulated in the imam-training issue—that the state's engagement with Britain's Muslim communities under the aegis of the Prevent program was designed to control how Britain's Muslims think and what they believe. It soon became clear that the project of promoting moderate, mainstream, authentic Muslim voices signified state intervention in the realm of religion for the purposes of national security, and that the very category of mainstream or authentic Islam referred to an interpretation of the religion that agreed with UK government policy. It seemed that the authentic or true meaning of Islam and religion was not an essential, self-evident one after all. In fact, what Islam "really meant" turned out to be highly political.

This was especially the case in the arena of foreign policy. Expectations were high that the MCB would faithfully reproduce the official state discourse on religion, Islam, social cohesion, and security. To an extent it did, but as the Prevent strategy went into action, no one, including the MCB, seemed to know exactly what the implications of the program were for freedom of speech regarding the country's foreign policy, especially in the Middle East. While declaring that "Muslims balance a sense of allegiance to the global Muslim community with the responsibilities of citizenship to their nation-state," the council also "deprecates the patronizing and pressuring attempts for Muslims to make declarations of loyalty" to British foreign policy (MCB 2007, 9–10). The problem clearly seemed to be a mixing of religious interpretation with loyalty to the state. Matters would come to a head when, in March 2009, the MCB refused to condemn one of its board members, Daud Abdullah, for signing a declaration "which advocated attacks on the [British] Navy if it tried to stop arms intended for Hamas being smuggled into Gaza" (Slack 2009a). Abdullah, Deputy Secretary General of the MCB, and also a member of the steering group of MINAB, was one of 90 Muslim leaders who had signed the "Istanbul Declaration." The declaration contained the following injunction: "the obligation of the Islamic nations is to regard the sending of foreign warships into Muslim waters, claiming to control the borders and prevent the smuggling of arms into Gaza, as a declaration of war, a new occupation, sinful aggression. This must be rejected and fought by all means and ways" (Slack 2009b). By late March of 2009, Hazel Blears had stated that the MCB's relations with the government would be suspended until the MCB took a stand against Abdullah. In a letter to the MCB dated March 13, 2009, Blears wrote "if it is the case that a senior office holder in MCB signed the declaration made at the Global Anti-Aggression Campaign event, I would expect the MCB to ask the individual concerned to . . . resign his post" (Blears 2009c). When the MCB refused, the government turned on the MCB. It was reported that going forward, "mosques and local Muslim community groups are to be given money and direct access to government ministers under a radical plan to isolate" the MCB and "undermine its standing among British Muslims" (Kerbaj 2009).

As the MCB worked through its problems with the Blair government, the organization emerged as one of the most vocal critics of the Prevent program. In a 2008 speech at the University of Cambridge, Muhammed Abdul Bari complained about the "disproportionate focus on this community through the lens of security" (Abdul Bari 2008, 3). Nor did Abdul Bari mince words regarding the creation of the "theology board" at Cambridge: "for too long now, British Muslims have been viewed by this government through the narrow prism of security. British Muslims . . . have every right to peacefully disagree with government policies if they wish and they do not need to be re-programmed by a government-approved list of theologians" (Muslim Council of Britain 2008). UK government engagement with the country's religious communities under the seemingly innocuous, neutral category of mainstream or authentic thus encountered a serious problem: the perception was growing that *authentic* understandings of Islam seemed to mean interpretations of the religion that agreed with British foreign policy.

This had very real implications for Muslim organizations in Britain, as mainstream or moderate Islam became the ticket to government funding. There is evidence to suggest that Prevent created a number of unintended consequences concerning religion and identity. The emphasis on religion in the Prevent program led to a decrease in funding for programs promoting racial equality, so "South Asian organizations are successfully accessing Prevent funding through emphasizing the Muslim aspect of their identity" (HC 65, 19). The head of Britain's Institute for Community Cohesion remarked that "the irony is that the Prevent agenda reinforces Muslim identity because it only approaches Muslims through their faith . . . it creates the impression that the only thing the government is interested in is their Muslimness" (21). This in turn divided Muslim organizations against each other and also created rifts between and among Britain's different faith communities. As Abdul-Bari put it, "many non-Muslim faith groups envy us that we are getting lots of money. At the same time, it is also creating internal division in our community" (7). Indeed, there is good evidence to support this. In his presentation of written evidence to a House of Commons review of the Prevent program, Dr. Indarjit Singh of the Network of Sikh Organizations wrote of Prevent, "religion has been brought into it and there are constant references to Islam . . . other communities are ignored . . . that (Muslim organization) has been getting additional funding for all sorts of projects and they therefore see themselves in a sort of favored status as a result of radicalisation" (17–19). The National Muslim Women's Advisory Group argued that "minority Muslim groups, with track records for large output but without the backing of the favoured organizations (such as the MCB) are more often than not ignored and marginalized from funding" (167).

The Prevent program also confused community cohesion with security measures. Suleman Nagdi, Federation of Muslim Organizations, argued that "tensions between faith communities have surfaced" because of the "confusion between the Prevent and Community Cohesion agenda" (85). One member of the Northwest England Ulema Council, a member organization of the MCB, remarked that "we are seeing a climate of suspicion were young men going to the mosques on a regular basis seems to cause concern— Prevent seems to have made us fearful and anxious of each other" (153). The fact that PREVENT programs were directed specifically to Muslim community organizations not only raised the perception among Muslims that they are a "suspect community" but also aroused the resentment of other communities, undermining the very social cohesion the initiative was meant to foster (Choudhury and Fenwick 2011, ix).

In addition, the Prevent program failed to convince the relevant audience. The communities surveyed did not share the government's opinion on what should count as an existential threat to Britain. One report claims

Muslims are told there is a 'severe' threat to the UK from international terrorism That they must help prevent and yet, for most in this study, this does not seem to resonate with their everyday experience . . . this contributes to a perceived disconnection between state insistence on the primacy of the threat from international terrorism and communities, where a wider range of social issues . . . are identified as posing a more real and concrete threat to society. (Choudhury and Fenwick 2011, vii)

Indeed, "a significant theme in interviews and focus groups across all case study areas is the disjuncture between state perceptions of threat and community perceptions of threat" (11). Moreover, those who work in Muslim community organizations have an incentive to exaggerate the threat of international terrorism to receive state funds (Choudhury and Fenwick 2011). This is important because it suggests that Muslim communities cannot express themselves in any manner outside of a security or counterterror framework.

State pressure on Muslim communities to reform their religion in the name of national security heightens religious identification that undermines community cohesion, revealing the central contradiction in New Labour's desire to promote a more robust role for religion in the public sphere. While political elites take pains to separate religion from political ideology, and thus regulate religion to the non-political, private sphere, the policy mechanisms through which this is attempted actually reinforce religion as a phenomenon of group identification that can strain the fabric of the central political unit, the community. This creates a cycle of contradiction in which moderate versions of religion need to be identified and reinforced, precisely to counteract the effects of the securitization of religion.

Finally, the Hizb ut-Tahrir was particularly outspoken in its resentment toward the British state for intervening in Islam. Taji Mustafa, a spokesman for the group, remarked that "whether it is the proposed state citizenship indoctrination for children in madrassas, or the new Imam board, the British government's interference in the Muslim community and matters of Islam is unprecedented in comparison with any other religion or community" (Ford 2008). Mustafa went on to say "the government would like nothing more than to have credible figures pronounce that opposition to their foreign policy is tantamount to heretical extremism. Their problem has been to find credible figures to do their work" (Casciani 2008). The group also condemned with vitriol other Muslim organizations that took the government bait. In a 2004 "letter to the Muslim community" in Britain, they wrote:

we send you this letter in light of plans recently revealed for the Muslim community in Britain and the requests made by so-called 'Islamic' organisations to Muslims and Mosques to spy on Muslims for the government. These plans have been made public as the British government wishes to increase the pressure on the Muslims living under their authority. They want us to spy on each other and divide us into 'loyal moderates' and 'disloyal extremists' according to their corrupt capitalist criteria. (Hizb ut-Tahrir 2004)

By 2009, the government had received an avalanche of criticism over the Prevent program. In 2009 the British House of Commons ran an in-depth investigation that produced over 300 pages of written and recorded testimony from think tanks, Muslim organizations, academics, government officials, city councils, police associations, and others. A number of important themes surfaced, all of which pointed in the same direction: Prevent had major flaws and would have to be fundamentally recast. Many participants reported that their constituents, coworkers, and fellow citizens could not shake the perception that the program was being used to spy on the country's Muslim communities. Another common complaint was that by calling the program Prevent, the government had given the impression that the Muslim community was inherently vulnerable and susceptible to extremist messages. In other words, the program had singled out Britain's Muslim community as a community at risk; a community under suspicion; a community whose members, if not carefully monitored and attended to, could slip into extremism at any moment.

The main problem lay with the very concept of moderate or mainstream Islam itself. For one thing, those individuals or communities perceived as belonging to the mainstream—or at least according to Prevent's understanding of that word—were seen by others as having sold out to the establishment. The Federation of Muslim Organizations noted, for example, that in many cases younger more radical British Muslims see those who belong to the "mainstream" as "legitimate targets" (HC 65, 23). It was also very difficult for the state and the organizations that worked with it to determine where moderate or authentic Islam ends and radicalism or "violent extremism" purportedly begins. The Islamic Society of Britain noted that "tackling extremism *per se* through the Prevent program will malign orthodoxy and conservatism, both of which are common given the migratory patterns of British Muslims" (HC 65, 196). Finally, the very classifications of Islam the British state had used invited accusations of hypocrisy. As the National Mus-

lim Women's Advocacy Group reported, "there seems to be quite a significant amount of analysis into ideologies that are fundamentally the fuel for
violent extremists and yet many organizations that have these same identified ideologues are not only being supported, but in some cases funded as
well" (168). The British state seemed to be manipulating religious categories,
and flying blind while doing it.

Moreover, Prevent's focus on religion and bringing religion into counter-
terrorism work created fractures between and among Britain's faith communities and undermined national community cohesion, the very thing it was
meant to foster. Dr. Indarjit Singh, of the Network of Sikh Organizations,
Britain's largest representative body of Sikhs, remarked that "the involvement
of religion in a nebulous way . . . suggests religion is a problem," pushing aside
hard won efforts at interfaith dialogue (18). Another NGO argued, reflecting
a common outcome of securitization, "the formulation of the PVE policy
along religious lines has created both inter and intra-ethnic fractures . . . and
have only served to exacerbate a politics of "Us and Them" (184).

For all of the time and effort the British government had spent on trying to find just the right way to describe the threat accurately and frame
the Prevent strategy to appeal to multiple relevant audiences, in the end the
program brought religious groups in to the public sphere exclusively within
the context of security. This happened at both the level of the state and civil
society. The MCB argued that "it was an error to have contaminated the
way a department like Communities and Local Government is publicly perceived by placing national security concerns in its orbit" (152). It also happened at the level of civil society. As the Islamic Society of Britain argued,
"the twinning of the 'shared values' agenda with Prevent . . . confuses the
shared values agenda with a security paradigm" (193). The Labour government thus attempted to merge its desire to bring religion in to the public
sphere in the name of cohesive communities, while at the same time making
"religion part of the solution" to the problem of "violent extremism." At the
House of Commons testimonial, a representative of the UK's Somali Family
Support Group summarized the problem quite well: "positioning a program
that denotes to fight violent extremism and help support and capacity-build
Muslim communities in one sentence spelt disaster from day one" (8).

SECURITIZATION'S FAILURE

By late 2009, having taken on board the numerous criticisms, the British
government prepared an overhaul of the Prevent strategy. Moderate and

mainstream Islam had proven poor classifications on which to base a program of outreach and engagement to the country's Muslim representative organizations and communities. Owing to the widespread resistance from civil society groups the government also discovered that religion could not be brought into the public sphere as a building block of cohesive communities at the same time that the state attempted to actively promote acceptable versions of religion in the name of national security. The British state had denied its intention to intervene in religious and theological affairs from the very beginning, but the sum total of criticisms from a wide spectrum of British Muslim organizations, think tanks, and others made clear that in actual practice, the Prevent strategy ended up doing precisely this.

The House of Commons review of the Prevent program concluded that "many of our witnesses believed that the Government has overplayed the role of religion" in Prevent, and the House recognized that there had been "an excessive concentration on the theological basis of radicalisation in the Prevent programme" (31–33). The House also seemed willing to entertain the possibility that radicalism may have had more to do with structural factors such as socio-economic conditions rather than distorted religious ideas: "the causal link between recruitment and underlying socio-economic conditions leading to vulnerability seem to have been included" in the Prevent strategy "but not emphasized adequately enough by government," which preferred to "focus on security and religion" (25). The preponderance of the oral and written testimony given at the hearings showed beyond doubt that "the majority of our witnesses saw any attempt by Government to advise on 'wrong' or 'right' interpretations of Islam as unwarranted interference, or even a 'cynical experiment in social engineering'" (34). The House finally concluded that "the evidence therefore starts to suggest that, particularly with regard to young people, an approach to preventing violent extremism which seeks to promote 'legitimate' interpretations of Islam and decry others may not be the most effective" (37).

Unable to ignore the fact that the state had lost credibility, in 2010 the government announced it would change their approach. The government attempted to *desecuritize* religion by separating public sector initiatives designed to support community cohesion from counter-radicalization, policing, and security-related programs. The latter would still have an ideological component, but no longer would the British government blur the lines between religion and national security by attempting to promote one interpretation of Islam over another. In a 2010 speech to the Royal United Services Institute, the new home secretary, Theresa May, declared that the original Prevent strategy had "muddled up work on counter-terrorism with the normal work that needs to be done to promote community cohesion and participation. Counter-terrorism became the dominant way in which government and some communities came to interact. That was wrong and it alienated so many" (Travis 2010; see also Travis 2007).

In June 2011, the British government released its new Prevent strategy. Addressing matters of religion directly, the new strategy argued that Prevent must no longer "seem to pass judgment on faith or *to suggest only a particular kind of faith is appropriate or acceptable*" (Prevent 2011, 7). The government noted that in its consultations on Prevent "some expressed concern that the Government was involving itself in matters of faith in a way they believed was inappropriate" (Prevent 2011, 45). The report goes on to say that only in "certain well-defined and exceptional situations" will the government deal with matters of theology, largely because the government "must avoid seeming either to want or to endorse a particular kind of 'state Islam'" (51). The report also addressed head-on the distinction between religion as authentic faith and religion as ideology, arguing that the concept of ideology was never "sufficiently disaggregated" in terms of what it means, and who it does and does not refer to. Discursive and conceptual ambiguity of this type, the document stated, was in part responsible for the "misperception that the Government was taking upon itself the role of theological arbiter or that this part of Prevent means that Government is passing judgment on Islam itself" (50). Under the new approach the British government will not disengage from encouraging certain religious developments altogether; the point is that such efforts will henceforth be separated from security and counterterrorism work. The role of the government in dialogue with faith institutions, for example, "will be significantly different from its role in any other area" (63). Nonetheless, the strategy maintains, multifaith integration projects and interfaith dialogue should not be part of counterterrorism work; interfaith work must not be given a "security label" (30). The House of Commons went on to recommend that any further outreach on the part of the state to the country's Muslim communities be definitively separated from any police or counterterrorism work.

CONCLUSION

Following 9/11 and especially after the London bombings on 7/7, the British government encouraged the country's Muslim communities to play a more active role in promoting national security. Underpinning this approach was

New Labour's conviction that religious faith contributed to strong, resilient, and secure national communities. In order to incorporate religion into the public life of a secular Britain, the parameters of religion first had to be defined. This involved, first and foremost, drawing the distinction between true and false versions of Islam and the enlisting of associations to help define and develop the former, which became known as *moderate Islam*. As time passed, the British state intensified its engagement and raised its expectation, ultimately arguing that the promotion of moderate Islam in Britain in the name of national security was a social and political obligation.

A variety of programs were put into place, including imam training, theology boards, police training in religion, and traveling road shows. New Muslim representative organizations were created with the encouragement and funding of the state such as the Sufi Muslim Council and the Quilliam Foundation. Islamic Studies was declared a strategically important subject in British higher education. The British government undertook such measures in order to help bring into being a version of Islam that would reflect Britain's core values and strengthen the cohesion of its communities. National security depended in part on the strength of national religious faith, for as Hazel Blears had argued, those with the weakest understand of their own faith were the most vulnerable to violent extremism. A strategy of "theological confutation" was set into motion by the secular state. The solution to Britain's post–9/11 security crisis was not less religion, but more.

Over time, however, as the outlines of Britain's approach to religion and security became clear, cracks between to show between the country's Muslim representative organizations and the government, police, and security forces, and between and among the country's Muslim communities themselves. Something seemed wrong with the secular state's mixing of religious matters with issues of national security. The discourse surrounding religion and national security during this period implied that all British Muslims were potential security problems, and so the state must work with reputable Muslim community leaders to surveil, and, if necessary, control the development of Islam in Britain. But the problems went far beyond stigmatization. Indeed, by 2009–2010 the British House of Commons conducted a full review of the programs and found widespread resistance to Prevent's programs for a long list of reasons. Religious organizations—predominantly Muslim, but others, too—complained that the Prevent program "mixed up" initiatives meant to promote community cohesion with those meant to increase surveillance and intelligence gathering. The program also led many to exaggerate either the threat the country faced or the religious (as opposed to racial or ethnic) features of their own communities just to attract money from the state. Thirdly, programs such as the imam-training programs and the state-sponsored organizations that arose to carry out the state agenda on religion had little credibility with the country's Muslim populations as a whole. The sum total of this led to a situation in which the secular British state was widely perceived as seeking to manipulate religion by encouraging certain interpretations of Islam over others for reasons of national security. To make matters worse, one's loyalty as a Briton was contingent on the extent to which one accepted these state-sponsored interpretations of the faith.

The British state thus securitized religion at the domestic level analysis by encouraging the construction of moderate Islam as a referent object for security. Moderate Islam referred to a version of that religion that not only eschewed violence but embraced British core values such as respect for multiculturalism, secularism, tolerance, and community cohesion. Britain's domestic securitization of religion failed because civil society organizations resisted the intrusion of a secular state into theological affairs and resented the implication that loyalty to the state was contingent on the content of one's religious beliefs. As the House of Commons hearings indicated, the state-sponsored version of Islam seemed to have little legitimacy among Britain's Muslim populations, even among those who felt that balancing faith and citizenship presented no real problems at all. The categories introduced in public discourse—violent extremism, radical Islam, moderate Islam, British Islam—simply smacked too much of state manipulation.

Ultimately the British state was unable to convince the relevant audiences that radical extremist ideology was an existential threat to the country's communities and that religion should play a role in counterterrorism and security work. In the aftermath of the House of Commons hearings, as the new government of David Cameron came into power, the state took measures to desecuritize religion by separating the state departments designed to encourage religion's role in public life to promote community cohesion from those responsible for security and intelligence work.

The struggle over the relationship between religion and national security in Britain continues. The Cameron government has sought to separate surveillance and intelligence-gathering programs from those meant to promote integration and community cohesion. The government has, on the other hand, taken a harder line against extremism, greatly expanding what that category includes. For example, while the New Labour approach focused on preventing violent extremism, the new government seeks to challenge even those who teach that Islam is incompatible with democracy. As one

Whitehall official put it, "we want to move away from just challenging violent extremism. We now believe that we should challenge people who are against democracy and state institutions" (BBC News, 2009). Indeed, the new strategy would "widen the definition of extremists to those who hold views that clash with what the government defines as shared British values" (Dodd 2009). Having taken measures to desecuritize religion by separating state engagement with religious organizations from departments involved in domestic intelligence and security work, the British state continues to take fire from some Muslim organizations. The Cameron government's extension of the category of "extremist" seems particularly disturbing. As the MCB wrote in a statement, "we are faced with a situation where a Muslim will be deemed extremist if defined so by neoconservative think-tanks" (Muslim Council of Britain 2011). Farooq Murad, Secretary General of the MCB, wrote in reaction to the revised Prevent strategy, "for Muslims security has become the only consideration on the agenda. It contains the implicit assumption that Muslims are less able to function in an open democracy than other people . . . it sends a very negative message to the community and is likely to increase Islamophobia" (Muslim Council of Britain 2011).

In conclusion, British attempts to securitize religion by establishing closer links to religious organizations and promoting moderate Islam after 9/11 failed. The initial objective of the British state was to help create, fund, and then rely on British Muslim organizations to promote a certain interpretation of Islam. The secular state justified this engagement with religion through the promotion of national security through community cohesion. Even as the Cameron government continues to redefine the scope of its categories and tinker with how to engage with religion in the public sphere, the lesson of Britain is clear: domestic-level securitizations of religion are prone to failure because they rely on the creation of referent objects such as *moderate Islam* or *real religion*. These referents themselves quickly become objects of contestation among civil society for a host of reasons, forcing the secular state to retreat, retrench, and rethink its public engagement with religion.

4 ✦ France

Securitization and Laicite

In Britain, New Labour welcomed religion into the public sphere as a necessary ingredient for the formation of secure, cohesive communities. In France, however, both the secular left and the Republican right/center right have long held that that the more religion enters into the public sphere, the more this will threaten the values of liberty, equality, and fraternity that underpin the security of the nation. In a 2003 address to a conference of ambassadors in Paris, for example, former Prime Minister Dominique du Villepin argued that the global rise of religion as an identity marker for individuals and communities was a reaction to globalization. Around the world, Villepin explained, peoples turned to religion for a more authentic and meaningful identity in the face of cultural, political, and social homogenization. The increasing turn to religious identities is a matter of national security, for identity is unstable, unpredictable, and "may crystallize at any moment, leading to confrontation between different groups" (Villepin 2003). Unchecked, religious identity or communitarianism threaten *laicite* and national security. It is for this reason that, according to one observer, "the formation of religious and ethnic communities . . . is dissuaded, if not constitutionally forbidden" in France (Samers 2003, 354). Such long-standing reservations about religion's role in the public sphere help to explain the controversy surrounding Sarkozy's campaign for "positive *laicite*"—the idea that religion must be brought in to public life and closer to the "public power" in the name of national security. Indeed, judging by the national reaction, *Le Figaro* reported, Sarkozy seemed to have "broken every taboo" about religion and its place in modern France with his notion of positive *laicite* (Bastiere 2008).

The concept of positive *laicite* lies at the heart of the French state's securitization of religion. It is under this heading that the French state, like Britain, seeks to train its imams, bring religion into its national security discourse and practice, call on the academy to produce knowledge about religion and Islam, and reach out to Muslim representative organizations as partners in the effort to deliver this agenda or, when necessary, to help create such organizations. But as in Britain, too, France's domestic securitization of religion has met with widespread resistance from civil society and provides another example of securitization's failure at the domestic level of analysis. To truly understand this one must first take into account the wider context of the new relationship that has emerged between religion and national security in France under positive *laicite*.

RELIGION AND NATIONAL SECURITY IN FRANCE

As in Britain, France's securitization of religion at the domestic level of analysis occurs in the wider context of a post–9/11 expansion of the national security agenda. France released White Papers on National Security in 1972, 1994, and again in 2008. Like the 2008 National Security Strategy of the United Kingdom, the 2008 French White Paper for Defense and National Security signifies an expansion of French thinking about the nature of threat and national security policy. "The world has radically changed" since the end of the Cold War, the strategy notes and so a "new appraisal was in order" (Defense et Securite Nationale 2008, 3). The paper reflects the French understanding of globalization as portending a return to identity politics, speaks of the battle of ideas, and warns against a clash of civilizations. In contrast to the 1994 White Paper, the 2008 French plan thus reflects an understanding of an expanded field of security that goes beyond the traditional military and defense sectors. In the report, "security interests are appraised globally without restricting the analysis to defence issues . . . the scope of national security includes the defense policy, but it is not limited to it." Rather "*knowledge and anticipation*" are new strategic priorities (5).

"Knowledge and Anticipation"—what the paper will later refer to as "knowledge-based security"—represents a major new topic for the French security establishment alongside traditional ones such as nuclear deterrence, conflict prevention, the transatlantic and NATO alliances, and others. The report goes on to claim, "if the pivot of the 1972 White Paper was deterrence" and "that of the 1994 White Paper was force projection," knowledge-based security lies "at the heart of the new dispensation" (11).

It is in this context of knowledge-based security that religion appears. Knowledge is the first line of defense in an uncertain and unstable world in which religious identity can crystallize at any moment. To deal with this and other possibilities the state needs to be one step ahead in its intelligence gathering, regional/area-specific knowledge, cultural intelligence, diplomatic education, analysis of future trends ("horizon-scanning") and information management. Knowledge-based security is critical in a globalized world in which "threats . . . are increasingly interconnected" and "sudden surges in tension, driven by the speed with which information, images and ideas travel—as we have seen in the religious sphere in recent years—are creating a particularly unstable environment conducive to flare-ups of violence" (55).

Reflecting the important role of religion in France's new concept of knowledge-based security, the French Ministry of Foreign Affairs (MFA) created the Center for Religions in June 2009. The task of the center is to integrate religion into the strategic thinking of France's security and diplomatic establishment. As French Foreign Minister Bernard Kouchner told *Le Monde*, "we have integrated demographics, the environment, and pandemics into our strategic thinking . . . why not religion?" (Marquand 2009b). The head of the new office, Joseph Maila, made the connection between religion and the new French approach to national security explicit, remarking in an interview that "the conclusion of the white paper on foreign and European policy of France have shown that the classical view of international relations that is based solely on the parameters of political power . . . is exceeded" and so now religion must take its place in the national security thinking (Globalist 2010). The new office of Religion in the MFA will train diplomats in religion, and will be attached to the MFA's Directorate of Forecasting. "Our primary mission is to provide information, analysis and reflection in religious matters" in order to anticipate future threats to national security (Globalist 2010). The creation of the Department of Religions is necessary because France must "win the battle of ideas" and this requires widening the traditional parameters of security and paying particular attention to religion as a driver of both state and nonstate actors. Not surprisingly, counterterrorism is at the top of the agenda. As the French White Paper on Terrorism and National Security claims, echoing the discourse of both Sarkozy and Blair, "to splinter our societies, global terrorism resorts to exploiting Islam for political purposes, scorning the precepts of peace and tolerance taught by this religion. . . . It is the unity and cohesion of our country that protect us from the clash of civilizations into which global terrorism seeks to drag us" (La France Face au Terrorisme 2006, 123).

If religion is to be tackled, however, national security can no longer be left "solely to the specialized counter-terrorism security agencies" (97–98). Just as in Britain, the new approach to French security seeks to introduce matters of religion into domestic counterterrorism and police work. In particular, instruction of "magistrates, police forces, and gendarmes" must "incorporate knowledge of the social and religious realities of contemporary French society" and the ideological references of terrorist groups (98). Recalling Hazel Blears's remark that the greatest threat to British national security comes from those with the weakest understanding of their faith, the French strategy argues that "only an objective and detailed knowledge of religious traditions and texts can make it possible for young people of all faiths to avoid falling under the sway of extremists distorting the message of their faith, by applying historical, political and social analysis to religions" (103–4). This new dimension of the *esprit de défense* will operate on the domestic level of analysis and must be "widely promoted and shared throughout French society" (98).

After 9/11 we thus begin to see religion incorporated into the strategic thinking of the French national security community. Similarly to Britain, the post–9/11 security climate widened the French conception of national security and helped to push the state into ever deeper engagement with religious ideas and actors at the domestic level of analysis.

SECURITIZATION OF RELIGION CONFRONTS *LAICITE*

As with all the cases in this book, France's moves toward increased state engagement with religion as a matter of national security proved controversial. France has a long tradition of what one writer has termed "assertive secularism" (Kuru 2009). Assertive secularism seeks to guard French state and society from the intrusion of religion. To do so, it seeks to discourage religious signs and symbols from the public sphere. Assertive secularism of the French variety can be contrasted with passive secularism. Passive secularism adopts a more tolerant attitude toward religion, welcoming religion into the public sphere in the name of toleration, multiculturalism, and pluralism. For passive secularists, the state should refrain from intervention in religious affairs rather than take an active role to ensure religion's absence in the public sphere. These two very different versions secularism continue to compete with each other in present-day France, and this can most clearly be seen in the debates surrounding the *foulard* affair (Kuru 2009).

Following September 11, France faced the same security conundrum that the U.S. and Britain did: a new approach was needed that would enable the state to conduct a war of ideas on its own terms while not alienating those whose support was needed most. As the U.S. and Britain struggled with how to handle the "irreducibly religious element" of the War on Terror without being seen to intervene in religious affairs or manipulate religion, Sarkozy developed his own approach to the problem that he termed "positive *laicite*" or positive secularism. The purpose of Sarkozy's positive secularism was to help justify and legitimate the secular state's intensified engagement with religious actors for reasons of national security. Yet positive *laicite* proved controversial in France's post–9/11 social and political climate, a climate that favored a retrenchment of the country's traditional, more assertive form of *laicite* to combat what was perceived as a growing threat represented by religion.

What is Sarkozy's conception of positive *laicite*, or positive secularity? Not synonymous with passive secularism, positive *laicite* envisions a more active role for the state in religious matters while maintaining France's traditional wariness of communitarian projects. Positive secularity or positive *laicite* refers to both policy prescriptions and wider change in attitude about religion in French society. As Sarkozy remarked, positive secularism "does not consider religions as a danger, but as an asset" (Samuel 2008). Sarkozy elaborated on the concept in a 2005 book entitled *The Republic, Religions, the Hope* (Sarkozy 2005), as well as in much-publicized speeches at the Lateran Palace in Rome (2007e) and later in Saudi Arabia (2008a). In attempting to stress what made his approach to religion unique, Sarkozy assembled an awkward ideological construction, claiming that although "the roots of France are essentially Christian," secularism "is no longer contested by anyone"; still, on the other hand, "secularism cannot be the negation of the past . . . secularism has no power to cut France's Christian roots . . . to pull the root is to lose the meaning, is to weaken the cement of national identity" (Sarkozy 2008e). The goal of positive secularism is to facilitate the "daily life of the great spiritual currents" for "the long secular republic has underestimated the importance of spiritual aspiration" (Sarkozy 2008e). Positive secularism is necessary to keep the clash of civilizations "in a state of fantasy" rather than becoming "a most tragic reality" that will threaten international peace and security (Sarkozy 2008e).

Whatever one may think of the coherence of Sarkozy's discourse on religion, positive *laicite* is important to the story I tell here, precisely because it created the conditions for the French state to interact more openly with religion in the name of national security. Joseph Maila, head of the Foreign Ministry's newly established Center for Religions, has claimed exactly this (Heneghan 2009a; 2009b). In the policy realm, positive secularism allows the French state to take an active role in encouraging the development of religion at the domestic level of analysis, and in the French situation, this refers to Islam. Indeed, after 9/11 and while still minister of the interior, Sarkozy, not unlike Tony Blair, pushed the state to take a more active role in bringing religion in to the public sphere for reasons of national security by supporting the training of imams, modifying the laws that define religious organizations, subsidizing the building of mosques, and by embarking on the country's most ambitious plan to yet to create a new umbrella Muslim organization to serve as the official interlocutor between France's Muslim communities and the state. As one newspaper observed precisely, "concerns over the rise of Islamic extremism have led [France] to take a more and more active role in the affairs of the Muslim community in recent years" (Charlton 2005).

To be sure, the French state had long cultivated a relationship with Muslim representative organizations. Some of this history is discussed later. Yet previous attempts to establish formal relationships between the state and religion were meant to soften and/or appease the voices of Islam in France. In contrast, Sarkozy's positive secularism sought rather to *amplify* a particular version of Islam—a moderate, modern, French Islam—in the name of national security. "I have called for positive secularism," for "it would be madness to ignore religion," Sarkozy claimed in 2008 (Marquand 2008). A U.S. embassy cable reported that in attempting to go beyond both traditional forms of *laicite*, the Sarkozy government attempted to actively and explicitly create a "'public' (that is, officially recognized and supported) French Islam" that will separate religion and politics for reasons of national security (Pekala 2007).

Additional sources provide a valuable outsider's perspective on Sarkozy's experimentation with *laicite*. They help to illustrate how positive *laicite* represents an attempt to address both horns of the difficult dilemma posed by religion. In a 2007 meeting with U.S. embassy one official from the French

Foreign Ministry referred to the "bind" that France finds herself in "between keeping itself sealed off from the religious activities of citizens and its responsibility to monitor potential radicalization that could lead to terrorist acts" (Pekala 2007). Reminiscent of the case of Britain, Sarkozy sought to "modify the relationship between state and religion" in order to "harness the community-building capacity of faith-based organizations, while also—in connection with Islam—reducing the potential spread of political fundamentalism" (Pekala 2007). In the same meeting, Laurence Marion, the civil rights and public liberties advisor to the prime minister, told U.S. officials that "the Sarkozy administration was keen on finding ways to 'support faith-based groups' while at the same time 'not radically departing from the tenets'" of France's 1905 law (Pekala 2007).

Such comments illustrate very well the wider post–9/11 conundrum faced by all three states discussed in this book. Following 9/11 Western states must engage with religion more than before in the name of national security, yet doing so entails a number of risks. Sarkozy's conception of positive secularity, like community cohesion in Britain or, as we will see like "smart power" in the U.S., was a way of dealing with this dilemma. In the case of France, positive secularity required that the French state reach out to its Muslim representative organizations and help form new ones. On the other hand, greater engagement with religion in the public sphere is widely seen as a threat to the fundamental principle of assertive secularism. Resistance to positive secularism comes, in fact, from all sides of the political spectrum, including some Muslim organizations themselves. France thus finds herself pressured, on one hand, to insulate herself from religion so as not to endanger the traditional parameters of *laicite,* but on the other hand unable to ignore religion in public life for reasons of national security.

This remainder of this chapter is about the French experience in navigating this difficult problem. I begin with a brief review of the history of Muslim representative organizations in France, highlighting the creation of a new, larger umbrella organization after 9/11. In the course of this discussion I focus on how through such organizations the French state attempts to encourage and channel the development of a particular form of Islam itself in the name of national security. In particular I trace how Muslim representative organizations are expected, through imam-training programs and in other ways, to help incubate a moderate, modern, French version of Islam. Such a French version of Islam is a referent object for security deemed worth protecting, for it represents an interpretation of Islam that is amenable to *laicite* and, in the eyes of the state, hostile to the politico-religious project of communitarianism.

HISTORY OF FRENCH MUSLIM ORGANIZATIONS

France has a long history of encouraging and even sponsoring the emergence of official representative religious organizations to serve as interlocutors with the state. This is not inconsistent with France's traditional understanding of *laicite*. As one scholar of French Islam has observed, "the French state has never interpreted *laicite* to require that the state avoid involvement in the affairs of religious groups. If a religion achieves a presence in the public sphere, then the state considers it necessary that there be a single 'privileged interlocutor'" (Bowen 2004, 47).

The construction of the Grand Mosque of Paris in 1926 symbolizes the beginning of formal state recognition for Islam in France. From the beginning, the Grand Mosque of Paris served a double function. First, it was built to honor North African and black African soldiers who had fought and died for the mother country during World War I. Such soldiers were not only drawn from France's overseas colonial territories but also from the large pools of industrial, factory laborers inside France herself. In addition to serving as a memorial to these fallen soldiers, the Grand Mosque also provided the French state with a convenient point of contact through which to communicate with—and to a large extent, closely monitor—the country's Muslim population. Such centralized contact was considered necessary as France's Muslim population had grown increasingly politically aware and restive. Following World War II, the administration of the mosque switched from Morocco to Algeria as the French state desired more oversight over the development of Algerian Islam both in France and abroad during Algeria's war of independence.

French Muslim communities grew larger and more diverse throughout the 1970s and as they did, tensions began to emerge between and among them. For some, questions arose as to why the Grand Mosque should remain the sole representative of Muslim interests to the state. For others, the Grand Mosque remained an inaccessible tourist draw, irrelevant anyway to the lives of France's Muslims struggling with day-to-day issues of discrimination, social malaise, and unemployment. Nationalisms, too, played a role in such tensions, as France's other Muslim communities wondered why Algerian interests should get a wider hearing than their own.

In the 1980s and 1990s, the French government embarked on efforts to bring Islam even closer to the state, motivated by heightened concerns for national security. Indeed, the 1980s and 1990s are reported to have been "decades of great turmoil" for the French security establishment as increasing terrorist attacks in Paris during the 1990s at the height of the civil war in

Algeria created the perception among the French population that the security establishment was "helpless to stop terrorism" (Leach 2005). It was under these heightened security conditions and no small pressure from public opinion that the government of France intensified its efforts to bring Islam into closer contact with the state and began to encourage the development of a moderate French version of Islam.

By the 1980s two important Muslim umbrella organizations had come into being in France to compete with the Algerian-dominated Grand Mosque of Paris: the Union des Organisations Islamiques de France (l'OUIF), linked to the Egyptian Muslim Brotherhood and partly funded by Saudi Arabia, and the Federation Nationale des Musulmans de France (FNMF), whose constituency was dominated by Moroccans. In the 1990s Turkey began to post imams in France as a way to balance Algerian, Moroccan, and Egyptian influence over the development of French Islam (Pedersen 1999, 33). France's Muslim population thus absorbed multiple ideological and political currents from outside states. In so doing, French Muslims became more vocal, theologically diverse, and politically aware, while the French government found it increasingly difficult to navigate these competing voices and monitor them. The state had trouble identifying exactly which Muslim organization—and, by extension, which foreign interest—was organizing which form of Islamic mobilization, at precisely the time when Algerian Islamic groups on French soil (such as the FIS and later, the GIA) were becoming increasingly radical.

In response to this situation, then Minister of the Interior Pierre Joxe (1988–1991) established a new liaison organization in 1989 between the French state and the Muslim community, the *Conseil de Reflexion sur L'Islam en France,* or CORIF. Unfortunately for Joxe, the CORIF suffered from a serious legitimacy problem, for it its members were perceived to be too close to the government. After all, as one scholar notes, those individuals who were already close to the Ministry of the Interior were, by default, considered by it to be the most reliable representatives of the "voice of Islam" in France (Samers 2003, 358). Yet, despite its dubious legitimacy in the eyes of France's Muslim communities, the CORIF group did succeed in making headway on a number of issues. The group successfully established Muslim burial grounds in France, provided French soldiers of Muslim origin with halal food, and established a date for the beginning of Ramadan in France. Some saw these developments as bargaining chips used by the French state to secure the loyalty and support of the country's Muslim communities, much like the Grand Mosque of Paris after World War I. Whether or not this is true, the CORIF certainly served well a most important objective for the French state: "severing control of the Paris Mosque" from Algeria and balancing the power of the country's Muslim organizations against each other (358).

In addition, CORIF also served as a convenient and reliable surveillance mechanism. It provided the state with "immediate insight into the developments in religious practice," as well as "a platform through which it can act considerably in potential conflict situations" (Pedersen 1999, 37). Finally, from the perspective of the privileged who served on the organization's council, the CORIF provided "the development of Islam in France with a place to stand, an opportunity to develop from a legal space that does not refer the administration of Islam to Middle Eastern states" (38). In other words, although the CORIF suffered a legitimacy deficit in the eyes of many French Muslims, the organization did allow some French Muslim leaders and the Ministry of the Interior to gain more control over the development of Islam in France.

In the 1990s the French state intensified its efforts to balance the power of foreign influences over French Islam and monitor the religion's development. In 1993 Interior Minister Charles Pasqua moved aggressively to start yet another state-sponsored Muslim council, this time drawing publicly the distinction between "foreign Islam" and "French Islam." Pasqua decided to reverse Joxe's strategy: rather than severing Algerian control from the Grand Mosque of Paris, Pasqua decided instead to "entrench a domestic and domesticated Islam on French soil with the Algerian Grand Mosque of Paris as its cornerstone" (Fernando 2005, 3). Such an "entrenched" Islam in close communication with the state would be an Islam brought under control through engagement, and, it was hoped, left free to blossom on French soil without foreign interference. In 1999, Interior Minister Jean-Pierre Chevenement expanded the network of state-sponsored Muslim councils by signing a document "affirming the compatibility of Islam and the French Republic" with a number of Muslim organizations such as the UOIF (linked to Egypt's Muslim Brotherhood), the FNMF (linked to Morocco), and the Tabligh movement (linked to India) (Cesari 2004, 71). All of these groups were chosen to represent a more "modernist Islam" to the French state (Fernando 2005, 3).

The Creation of the *Conseil Francais du Culte Musulman*

Following 9/11, the largest and most important French Muslim representative organization, the *Conseil Francais du Culte Musulman* (CFCM), was initiated by then Minister of the Interior Nicolas Sarkozy in 2003 and consented to by a number of French Muslim organizations and the rectors of the Great Mosques of Paris and Lyon. The CFCM, whose first board of directors was not elected but chosen by the French state, is best seen as the culmination of the aforementioned attempts to include France's many Muslim communities at the "table of the republic" through the creation and support of an overarching representative Muslim organization. The purpose of the CFCM is to provide a single interlocutor to represent all of the country's main Muslim organizations, including the UOIF, the FNMF, as well as France's Tabligh, Turkish, and African Muslim communities. Also included in the CFCM are a number of influential mosques, imams, scholars, converts, and other public intellectuals (Amiraux 2003). The CFCM is responsible for exclusively religious tasks and duties such as new mosque construction, maintaining the Muslim calendar and the scheduling of feast days, as well as matters of halal food, burial, Muslim chaplains in the prisons and the army, and, as will be discussed shortly, imam training.

The CFCM is led by a president and vice president. At the council's formation in 2003, Dalil Boubakeur, Rector of the Grand Mosque of Paris, was chosen by the French state to lead the council as president and the decision was confirmed by the council's general assembly (Cesari 2004, 71). Two vice presidents were named: the first, Fouad Aloui of the OUIF; the second, Mohmed Bechari of the FNMF. Although the French government did handpick the council's first president and board of directors, it no longer has official say over who is to serve on the council of the CFCM, on its general assembly, or the board.

In addition, the CFCM has an executive committee, a board of management, and a general assembly. On the executive committee of the CFCM, for example, are the *Federation Nationale des Musulmans de France* (FNMF), supported by Morocco; the *Union des Organisations Islamiques de France* (UOIF), formed in 1983 and with ties to the Muslim Brotherhood; the *Institut Musulman de la Mosquee de Paris,* linked to Algeria; a French chapter of India's *Jama'at al Tabligh;* and other organizations representing the interests of Turkish, African, and French West Indian Muslim communities in France. As one might expect, given theological, cultural, and national differences among them, these organizations have competing agendas and often working at cross purposes. Competition is intense among the movements, especially between the governments of Algeria and Morocco, acting behind the scenes. The three largest organizations—the Grand Mosque of Paris (funded by Algeria), the FNMF (funded mostly by Morocco), and the OUIF (linked to the Muslim Brotherhood but funded by various sources)—

compete between and among each other for the organization's main executive leadership positions and for seats on its general assembly. Other, smaller Muslim organizations are represented, such as *Milli Gorus* and the *Comite de Coordination des Musulmans Turcs de France,* both of Turkish origin (Klausen 2005, 38). The idea behind the CFCM was to allow Islam in France to develop on French soil, independent of foreign influence. Nonetheless, the organization remains vulnerable to the pull of transnational ideological alliances that make up the global Muslim community (Eickelman 1997).

Why did Sarkozy create the CFCM? While minister of the interior, Sarkozy gave a series of policy speeches to the country's Muslim organizations in 2002 and 2003. "Islam is France's second religion," Sarkozy claimed in 2002. "It's also a religion whose diversity has to be understood . . . I appreciated both our excellent discussions and your desire to build *a French Islam and not Islam in France*" (Sarkozy 2002; emphasis mine). Sarkozy goes on to say "thanks to your work the government . . . has got an understanding of your faith and practices and has been convinced that Islam can accept the Republic's values" (Sarkozy 2002). He then registers his satisfaction that some agreement has been achieved "on the principle of creating a representative body of the Muslim faith," a need that "no one disputes" (Sarkozy 2002).

Most importantly, Sarkozy presents positive *laicite* as a vehicle to bring Islam out from the "darkness" and into the "light" of public participation and integration into the life of France. The creation of a representative Muslim organization would "facilitate the Muslim community's integration" into the French Republic. If such an organization were to be formed, "Islam will . . . be the religion which has voluntarily subjected itself to the most transparent and demanding democratic rules: throughout the world, this will be a spectacular sign of the modernity and vitality of this Islam of France" (Sarkozy 2002). Integration will also help to make Muslim communities more secure, instead of a "scapegoat" for the country's post–9/11 insecurities (Sarkozy 2002). Integration, the surest path to security, will thus demonstrate to the world that French Islam is prepared to be "modern"; according to Sarkozy, to be antimodern is to be "fundamentalist" and "stand in the way of the Republic's essential principles" (Sarkozy 2002). As Sarkozy later claimed, "we have worried about clandestine Islam, for being clandestine contributes to radicalization, whereas public existence contributes to integration and even . . . normalization" (O'Brien 2005, xx).

For Sarkozy, "radicalism" refers to "clinging" to radical ideas, such as the notion that "a faith has no authority over the values of the Republic" or that "Islam is incompatible with the Republic" (Sarkozy 2003b). As in Britain, the burden of responsibility is placed on the country's Muslim communities to reconcile their convictions with the limits of political obligation. As Sarkozy put it in a 2003 address to the UOIF, "at a time when the war in Iraq casts a long shadow . . . your gathering is duty-bound to present an image of integration, peace, serenity, and citizenship" (Sarkozy 2003b).

There was thus pressure placed upon the CFCM to articulate and help police the parameters of moderate, modern, French Islam. The very category of moderate Islam became something of a competition among the CFCM members. Take, for example, the UOIF. Depicted in French media as fundamentalist and even radical, the UOIF presents itself as a religious authority to France's Muslim population, often stressing its religious credentials by its connections to Egypt's Muslim Brotherhood. Nonetheless "the UOIF's ideological, if not organic, links to the Muslim Brotherhood are seen as a threat to the French Republic. In response, the UOIF has attempted to portray itself as the promoter of an Islam of 'citizenship', contesting the GMP's [Grand Mosque of Paris] monopoly on Islamic moderation'" (Caeiro 2005, 73). Sarkozy, too, presented the CFCM as a way to keep fundamentalist interpretations of Islam at bay; the term *fundamentalist* meaning, in the French context, those who would place their loyalty to Islam over their loyalty to the French state—over the values of the Republic.

There is little doubt that national security concerns lay behind Sarkozy's attempt to bring Islam closer to the state to help incubate a French version of Islam. As the U.S. ambassador to France observed, since the creation of the CFCM the French government has "leaned on the CFCM to ensure a prominent place for moderates," while "keeping the FMNF and UOIF within the CFCM helps keep fundamentalists within the fold and in dialogue with the [Government of France]" (Stapleton 2005a). According to a member of France's internal security service, part of the purpose behind the creation of the CFCM was "to counter the message and attractiveness of these self-proclaimed imams . . . the GOF was working to encourage the Muslim community to organize itself with a clearly French identity" (Stapleton 2005d). The CFCM thus serves as a mechanism by which to insulate Islamic consciousness in France and secure French Muslim society against the intrusion of ideologies promulgated by foreign state and nonstate actors.

For this larger goal to be achieved, groups such as the CFCM and UOIF are expected promote a particular vision of Islam itself. In the words of one scholar, Sarkozy intended that such groups "contribute to the formalization of 'good Islam' in France, disseminating a liberal doxa and marginalizing radical elements" (Caiero, 2005, 78). Cast in the language of securitization, the CFCM's members are thus expected to become *securitizing actors*. As Sarkozy put it in his closing remark in his 2003 speech to the CFCM, "the national community holds its hand out to you . . . you are now accountable for the image of every Muslim in France. Take the hand held out to you by the Republic. Do not disappoint it for the consequences would be huge" (Sarkozy 2003).

Imam Training

Imam training is an important plank in Sarkozy's conception of positive *laicite*. To accelerate the development of a moderate, French Islam commensurate with the Republic's values, the French state encouraged Muslim organizations and educational institutions across the country to participate in the training of imams. As of 2005, one French study identified about 1,000 imams in France, about half of which are of Algerian or Moroccan origin; of the number who are paid (about 45 percent), the Turkish government supports 60, Algeria supports 80, and Morocco 2 (Klausen 2005, 116). Although the number of imams in France is not large (smaller Britain may have about twice as many) imams have emerged at the center of France's efforts to encourage the development of an Islam of France. Following September 11, 2001, the new minister of the interior, Dominique de Villepin, announced that "the country must urgently begin training Muslim clerics in a moderate Islam that respects human rights and the republican code" (O'Brien 2005, xxi). Villepin feared that "under the cover of religion, individuals present on our soil have been using extremist language and issuing calls for violence" (Ford 2004). With the creation of the CFCM in 2003, imam-training initiatives took on a new urgency. Before long, the CFCM was tasked with developing an "officially recognized" curriculum for imams in France (Peter 2003, 20).

Other attempts were made to train imams, notably through a partnership between the Grand Mosque and the Catholic University of Paris sponsored by the Ministry of the Interior. A brief glance at the course curriculum for the largest program reveals that it aimed at political socialization, attempting not meant to only inform but also to shape an approach to faith more accepting of the Western social science approach. The diploma, titled *Religions, Laicite, Interculturalite*, includes instruction in French history, the history of secularism, Enlightenment thought, Rousseau, Voltaire, and French citizenship (Yahmid 2009). In each of the pillars of the training program we find an emphasis on the history of republican values, a stress on not only the rights but also the obligations of religions in France, and the matter of religion's "openness" and reception to change and transformation by encounter with the "critical" or human sciences. The Catholic Institute and the Grand Mosque were to divide the relevant intellectual labor: the Catholic Institute will focus in instilling the principles of *laicite* and steer clear of religion and theology; the Grand Mosque charged with teaching the Koran, Islamic law, and Muslim history, all the while steering clear of any political matters.

Indeed, a crucial part of the training and retraining of imams in France is to socialize them to separate religion from politics (Haddad and Balz, 2008). The goal of the French state is to fund the training of homegrown imams who, in the words of one Muslim leader, "will preach on the Koran and not on some political agenda" (Siemon-Netto 2003). Dalil Boubakeur, rector of the Grand Mosque of Paris and chair of the CFCM until 2008, has been quoted in this context as saying "we cannot accept Islam as a political movement, or an ideology of power making trouble among our youth" (Spicer 2002). Boubakeur later remarked "we must distinguish between real imams and subversives . . . imams in France should absolutely stop talking politics" (Ford 2004). According to Boubakeur, the Grand Mosque urges the over 100 imams in its supervision to "obey French law and refrain from political speech in mosques" (Stapleton 2005b). Thus while the French state claims no intrusion into theological matters, it is expected that in addition to regulating calendars, feast days, halal meats, and other practices, the CFCM, under the watchful eye of the Ministry of the Interior, will help to ensure that religion remains *spiritual* and not political.

Challenges to French Securitization of Religion

Just as in Britain, where the Blair government's experiment with religion as both a problem and a solution led to widespread resistance to perceived state intervention in theology, France's intensified engagement with religion under the banner of positive secularity also gave rise to a host of objections from France's Muslim communities. Many in France's Muslim community resented the attempts by the French state to create what was perceived to be a state-sponsored version of their faith. Positive *laicite*—greater involvement of the state in religious affairs for reasons of national security—came under fire for precisely the same reasons as Britain's Prevent program.

The first problem had to do with the French state's intrusion into religious matters and criticism of its widespread use of religious categories. Shortly after the formation of the CFCM, for example, a number of critics blamed Sarkozy for "constituting, through religion, a public body for the regulation of social problems" (Caeiro 2005, 80). In the wake of the 2006 riots in the country's *banlieus*, it seemed that the state's relentless use of religious categories had begun to take social effect. A year after the riots U.S. special representative for Muslim communities, Farah Pandith, traveled to France to meet with a wide swath of French Muslims, especially Muslim youth. The reports from that visit are instructive. One interesting finding is that despite Sarkozy's widespread use of the phrase an "Islam of France" and the widely popular notion of "Euro-Islam" as a *desideratum* for Muslim identity promulgated by Western academics, many of the participants were puzzled by the terms and reported little familiarity with the notion of European Muslim identity. At the same time, however, the religious category seemed to have gained some traction in how France's Muslims understood themselves. Sociologists on the visit reported that "they had observed a new dynamic in social identity—growing self-identification as 'Muslims' going hand in hand with growing use of the religious identifier 'The Muslims' by the mainstream majority" (Pekala 2007). It is therefore not surprising, as one scholar would report, that "by privileging the Islamic component of immigrant identity, the state was accused of practicing a 'reverse religious communitarianism' and of pursuing dubious electoral gains, as well as playing into the hands of the Islamist movements active in the French suburbs" (Caeiro 2005, 80). Thus, some French Muslim communities reported little attachment or familiarity with the notion of an Islam of France; they simply did not see themselves this way, even if the religious component of group identity had been heightened.

Forces from across the political ideological spectrum, however, challenged Sarkozy's incessant use of the religious category. For the right, Sarkozy was pandering to the Muslim community for votes with his newfound engagement with religion, while centrist politicians such as Francois Bayrou warned that "challenging secularism" with positive *laicite* "opened up a Pandora's box of latent problems." (McNicoll 2008). The left in particular accused Sarkozy of using religion as a distraction from social problems such as unemployment and widespread youth disengagement. It was precisely such disengagement, and not any religious alienation, the French left contended, that led to the *banlieu* unrest in the first place (McNicoll 2008). Such resistance to positive laicite in France's political establishment existed for some time. When Sarkozy first expressed his plan for positive *laicite* in his 2004 book, *The Republic, the Religions, the Hope,* both Prime Minister Dominique de Villepin and President Jacques Chirac vehemently disagreed with Sarkozy's approach (Charlton 2005). Sarkozy pushed the envelope further with his speeches in Rome and Saudi Arabia. Sarkozy's positive *laicite* generated an outcry that, if only briefly, united the country's left, right, and center, which came together to staunchly defend the tradition of assertive secularism against what was perceived to be greater state involvement in religion through positive *laicite.*

A second problem had to do with the legitimacy of the CFCM, how effectively it represents the country's Muslim population, and how close the organization should be to the state. For example, in the 2005 CFCM election the FNMF won 19 of 43 elected seats on the CFCM's administrative council. This was seen as a great victory for Sarkozy's moderate French Islam. Flushed with victory, FNMF president Mohamed Bechari claimed that he encouraged "modern Islam, contextualized Koranic interpretation, and obedience to the state" (Stapleton 2005c). Meanwhile, however, the OUIF and Grand Mosque of Paris each won 10 seats on the council, which represented a sharp decline in representation for the OUIF. In France, the OUIF is perceived as "fundamentalist" given its ties to the Muslim Brotherhood (but see Kepel 2004, 253 and ff.). Following the 2005 elections Sarkozy pointed to the OUIF's electoral losses as evidence of victory for "his strategy to moderate French Islam" (Stapleton 2005c). But the OUIF had come to resent the close connections between the CFCM and the French state. The organization's secretary general, Fouad Alaoui, complained that the organization lost supporters when it joined the CFCM in the first place, moving closer to the state and becoming more mainstream (Stapleton 2005c).

In addition, U.S. embassy documents paint a wider picture of general dissatisfaction with the CFCM beyond the 2005 elections. The CFCM's primary shortcoming is that it only speaks for the approximately 10 percent of French Muslims who are considered "practicing" (Stapleton 2005c). From the very beginning the organization could hold together "only through the heavy-handed efforts of the French state," according to then U.S. Ambassador Craig Stapleton, and the decline of the UOIF in the 2005 elections is "unlikely due to any substantial moderation on the part of extremist Muslims" but rather to the possibility that a number of the UOIF's members see their group as having "sold out" to the French government (Stapleton 2005c). Indeed, a number of members did split from the UOIF and went on to form their own competing organizations, such as the Union of Muslim Associations of Seine-St. Denis in Paris, which has not only been critical of the CFCM but managed to organize over 7,000 protestors against the publication of the infamous Mohammed cartoons in 2006. A spokesman for the Grand Mosque accused the UOIF's protest organizers of using the cartoon incident to discredit the CFCM (Stapleton 2006a).

The president of the FNMF, Mohamed Bechari, argued as well that French Muslim youth "largely reject community institutions, including the CFCM" because "organizations such as the French Council of the Muslim Faith have little credibility or influence on the street due to their affiliation with the state" (Stapleton 2006b). Bechari and a number of his colleagues were "particularly critical of Sarkozy's efforts to create an "official Islam" that "does not represent Muslims in France" (Stapleton 2006c). Another prominent Muslim leader, Soheib Benscheikh, a mufti from Marseilles, argued that the CFCM embodied France's state-led, postcolonial approach to Islam. By this Benscheikh seems to have meant that through the CFCM the French state sought to manage and control the development of Islam in France to prevent any dissent from arising within the country's Muslim communities. Many Muslim leaders in France shared Benscheikh's sentiments, prompting one scholar to report that "the paternalism charges denouncing the 'neo-colonial' attitude of the government towards the Muslim communities at large have been the most frequent attacks against the entire initiative" (Amiraux 2003, 1).

In the 2007 U.S. embassy meeting mentioned earlier, U.S. officials had asked whether there was a need for a "Europe-wide, authoritative, 'voice of moderation' able to provide information to ordinary, middle-class Europeans on matters of religious practice and Muslim history, science, art, culture, and identity" (Pekala 2007). The response from a number of "civil society interlocutors" was that such an attempt might be dismissed by Muslims "as yet another state-sponsored attempt to guide their religion" (Pekala 2007). Finally, the French national security establishment conceded that state involvement in religion may have backfired, undermining national security. The 2006 White Paper on national security policy, prepared by a working group under the direction of Prime Minister Villepin, reported that the state's "pretension to organize Islam according to a national model [with the 2003 creation of the French Council of the Muslim Faith]" was one of the main reasons for recent attempted terrorist attacks in France (La France Face au Terrorisme 2006, 33).

Dissatisfaction with the state's attempts to encourage the development of a homegrown, moderate, French version of Islam was directed not only to the state's attempt to organize Islam along official lines but at specific policies as well. One example is the program to train imams mentioned earlier. As in Britain, resistance to imam training does not stem from the idea of imam training per se, but from the perception that the state will control what imams preach. One imam from Strasbourg, Abdallah Boussouf, agreed that "Muslim imams in France should have a modern education"—ideally a university education in both social sciences and Koranic studies—for such an education is the best guarantee of the religion's "harmonious future existence within a modern and secular western state" (Henley 2004). In 2005 the Sorbonne and other public universities in France declined to take on the task of imam training out of concern for blurring the lines between state and religion while a number of French Muslim leaders argued that the programs represent an attempt by the French government to manufacture a style of Islam more amenable to state control (OneNews 2007). Thami Breze, president of the UOIF, remarked in 2004 that "they are dramatizing (the situation) . . . they are preparing the ground to set up a government institute to train imams, and we are against such government interference" (Ford 2004). The small number of students who did participate in the programs come only from the Grand Mosque of Paris, and "those affiliated with other French Muslim organizations, including the popular, more fundamentalist UOIF, do not participate" (Bryant 2008). According to Fouad Alaoui, first vice president of the OUIF, although his organization "has never been against the idea" of state-sponsored imam training, such courses are ultimately intended to "sway Muslims away from orthodox or traditional solutions to common social problems" (Schmidt 2007). Controversy over imam-training programs, funding for mosques, as well as infighting between and among various national factions vying for power have all taken their toll on the CFCM. In the most recent CFCM elections in 2011, two groups boycotted and the UOIF urged a delay in the vote. "As a result of the election crisis" one reporter noted, "dissatisfied Muslim leaders have started to drift away" from the CFCM (Heneghan 2011).

Broadly speaking, France's Muslim leadership was concerned that the CFCM, portrayed as a body responsible for the regulation of religious practices and rituals pertaining to everyday life, provided a vehicle for the state to push its own version of Islam. Many Muslim representatives, while they welcomed the opportunity to have their voices heard, felt that the CFCM was unrepresentative and sought to bring the theology of Islam under government control. Even the French national security establishment was keenly aware that the state's attempt to bring Islam under state surveillance was a main reason behind recent terrorist attacks in the country. As criticisms mounted from politicians left, right, and center, as well as many of France's Muslim community leaders, Sarkozy's conception of positive *laicite* was in danger.

Other religious organizations in France religious organizations came together to defend traditional *laicite*, too. The failure of a planned nationwide debate on positive *laicite* is a good example. Following the passing of a law to ban the full face covering (the niqab) in public places in 2011, the French Parliament planned a public session to debate secularism in France in April 2011. Sarkozy and the UMP envisioned a publicly televised national conversation on "how to organize religious practice so that it is compatible in our country with the rules of our secular republic" (France 24). The debate was to include discussion of the main planks of Sarkozy's positive *laicite*, including financing for mosques and the ideological backgrounds of the country's imams. But the event met with widespread objection. Some of the objections had to do with domestic politics, as when editorialists and pundits speculated that the debate was a move by Sarkozy to preempt Martine Le Pen's radical right party from appearing stronger on radical Islam and national security. France's religious organizations, however, representing Catholics, Jews, Buddhists, Hindus, and others, were strongly against the debate, fearing it would stigmatize religion, especially Islam. Seeking to calm those who feared the debate would stoke further anti-Muslim sentiment, UMP Secretary General Jean-Francois Cope reassured the country's religious communities that the debate would focus on positive *laicite* (Islam Today 2011).

What Cope did not seem to understand was that for France's national religious organizations, positive *laicite* was precisely the problem. At first glance one might expect large national religious associations to welcome such a debate as an opportunity to argue on a national stage for a greater role for religion in public life. On March 30, 2011, however, a number of prominent French religious leaders, members of the *Conférence des Responsables de Culte,* an interreligious group including Catholic, Protestant, Jewish, Orthodox, Muslim, and Buddhist leaders, appealed to Sarkozy to cancel the debate (Connexion France 2011). The group warned against "squandering the precious practice of laicite" (France 24, 2011). In its appeal, the *Conférence* defended the national tradition of *laicite* against Sarkozy's conception of positive *laicite* out of concern that the latter would allow the state to manipulate religion. Meanwhile, as happened in Britain, the prospect of closer relations between the state and religion that the national debate seemed to support raised fears that political loyalties were being called into question. The president of the CFCM, Mohammed Moussaoui, argued that the debate implicitly questioned the loyalty of French Muslims and because of this, the CFCM refused to participate (French Council of Muslim Faith, 2011). Over the row, about a dozen CFCM members tore up their party membership cards and joined the Socialists (Islam Today 2011).

CONCLUSION

After 9/11, both Britain and France adopted similar discourses and policies regarding religion, and especially Islam. Underpinned by New Labour's discourse that religion can be both a problem as well as a solution, the British state tried to bring religion into the public sphere through its Prevent program, which sought to encourage the development of moderate Islam by relying on Muslim representative organizations, promoting imam training, theology boards, or traveling road shows to disseminate the concept of moderate Islam to the general public. Such efforts failed because Britain's Muslim communities resented what they saw as state intrusion into religious matters and theological manipulation. Moreover, extensive House of Commons hearings revealed widespread frustration with the way in which the British state under both Blair and Brown sought to use a greater public role for religion for intelligence gathering and other domestic security purposes. Eventually, the securitization of religion in Britain failed as the Prevent program was substantively overhauled, the most notable change being a new, definitive separation between state-sponsored programs designed to encourage a greater role for religion in British public life with those designed to protect national security.

As in Britain, the national security discourse of France posited religion both as a security problem and a security solution. However, while in Britain this approach appeared in New Labour's discourse on religion and community cohesion, France's post–9/11 approach to religion and security was framed by Sarkozy's notion of positive *laicite*. As Britain's New Labour government sought to promote a national, moderate version of Islam that would help British Muslims to overcome their identity crises and the weak understandings of faith that threaten national security, so did France under Sarkozy explicitly promote the idea of a moderate, modern "Islam of France" in the name of national security. While Tony Blair relied upon important Muslim representative organizations such as the Muslim Council of Britain to assist in the national security project of promulgating and policing the parameters of moderate British Islam, so did Sarkozy encourage the formation of the CFCM, an organization, according to Sarkozy, "duty bound" to present to audiences in France and abroad an image of French Islam as modern, and moderate. In fact, while Britain relied heavily on government departments to accomplish this task, the French case placed far more emphasis—and therefore a much greater burden—on the country's Muslim organizations, especially the CFCM. The CFCM was *the* central component in Sarkozy's strategy to bring positive *laicite* into being. Yet the CFCM suffers from a legitimacy deficit both within its ranks and among many French Muslims; imam training and state funding for mosques remain controversial and have thus far failed to materialize as hoped; some Muslim leaders ridicule the very notion of an official version of French Islam. French Muslim organizations like the CFCM did not identify with the categories promoted such as *moderate Islam,* and perceived such descriptions as illegitimate creations of an unrepresentative network of organizations that had grown uncomfortably close to the state. Finally, on the eve of a 2011 national debate on the concept of positive secularity, France's main religious organizations appealed to the head of state to cancel the event, fearful that positive *laicite* could very well in practice lead to state manipulation of religion.

From these two cases a general conclusion can be drawn. Domestic securitizations of religion—cases in which secular states attempt to bring religion in to public life for reasons of national security—create a variety of forms of backlash and criticism. Because Britain and France ran their domestic securitizations of religion for the most part through Muslim representative organizations, resistance from such organizations suggests that state intervention in the religious sphere for purposes of national security is highly problematic. The reason for criticism and resistance does not lie in the fact that religion has some untouchable *sacred essence* that the state soils by its interventions. As a referent object for security, moderate Islam fails, but not because it misrepresents what the religion really means. There is no such referent for religion. Rather, domestic-level securitizations of religion fail because they are widely perceived to be an affront to the community's freedom of thought and interpretation by making one's interpretation of one's faith a matter of national security. Based on the available evidence, it appears that domestic securitizations of religion privilege religion or Islam as problematic elements of group identity because the group simply does not understand, in the words of Blair, what their religion "really means." Thus, domestic-level securitizations of religion are inherently problematic for secular states and are, it seems, particularly prone to failure.

5 ✦ The United States
"Islam Will Police Itself"

        As Britain and France experimented with ways to bring religion
into the public sphere at home, the U.S. began to grapple with the religious
dimensions of its new war on terror abroad. As chapter 2 demonstrated, all
three states understood themselves to be thrust in the middle of a war of
ideas that raged within Islam. The security of each nation, as well as Western
civilization and its neoliberal order, hung in the balance. Western nations
must take sides in this war of ideas, Bush, Blair, and Sarkozy argued; religion
could no longer be ignored. Taking sides in the war of ideas required state
engagement with religion in the public sphere more than before, a strategy
that stretched the Western state's familiar secular arrangements. In Britain,
Hazel Blears announced that the country must overcome its national squeamishness about religion, for religion must be dealt with openly in the name
of national security. If religion was part of the problem then it would be part
of the solution. In France, Nicolas Sarkozy cautioned that to ignore religion
was to threaten national security and the very cultural identity of France;
thus Sarkozy attempted to adjust *laicite* precisely to make space for religion
in the public sphere. From Britain and France, the message seemed clear:
states must put aside their secularist reservations, for after 9/11, national security required a new, hard-headed engagement with religion. Scholars of
global politics increasingly argued that religion should be brought back in
to international affairs in the post–9/11 world; ironically, Western national
security establishments couldn't agree more.

        There was a distinctively American version of this new willingness to openly engage with religion in the public sphere to protect national security. Thomas Farr, the United States' first director of the State Department's Office of Religious Freedom, called it a "new American Religious Realism" (Farr 2008). When interviewed for this book Farr explained that the new American Religious Realism referred to "calling things by their real names rather than the names that disguise what they really are . . . we have tended to use euphemisms for religion in US foreign affairs for a long time . . . we talk about 'culture' when we want to disguise the fact that we're talking about religion . . . religion is an aspect of international affairs that needs to be named as such" (Farr 2011). Farr went on to explain that "we need religious realism because the world is religious and it's the job of American policy to engage the world in America's interests" (Farr 2011). As this chapter shows, following 9/11, engaging the world in America's interests meant increased U.S. government engagement with religion abroad. Indeed, after 9/11 U.S. diplomatic, security, and defense establishments embarked on a multipronged effort to understand, engage, and influence religion more than ever before. The process evolved over time, and continues to evolve as of this writing. After a number of early setbacks over public diplomacy and Muslim World Outreach programs, the U.S. government increasingly incorporated religion into its strategic planning and international partnerships by supporting efforts to promote moderate Islam. Such programs were quite successful; indeed, from the battlefields of Afghanistan to the Defense Ministry in Indonesia to think tanks in Kuwait and Jordan, encouraging the development of moderate Islam proved a useful way to strengthen strategic alliances for national security.

This international securitization of religion—the instrumental use of religion by the U.S. to shore up alliances and partnerships abroad—contrasts with engagement with religion at the domestic level of analysis by the governments of Britain and France. In Britain and France the secular state engaged directly with its targeted Muslim communities, encouraging them to participate in the privileging of certain interpretations of their religion over others in the name of national security. In both cases, such efforts met with failure as nonstate actors resented the intrusion of the secular state into theological matters, rejected ideological categories such as *moderate Islam* precisely because they appeared to be created by the state, and generally disapproved of the public representation of their religion as a subject of national security. Both cases represent clear failures to convince relevant audiences of the general security argument: that Islam's "real meaning" was under existential threat from ideological distortion, requiring the state to push secularism to its limits in order to defend it. In both Britain and France, greater state engagement in religious matters did little to achieve a sense of security at all, but in fact accomplished quite the opposite: it threatened the very community cohesion it meant to foster (Britain) and led to a widespread criticism and rejection of positive *laicite* for fear it would lead to greater state manipulation of religion (France).

In contrast, the U.S. has, through a process of trial and error, found a way to use religion abroad as a way to solidify alliances for national security. Under the label of *smart power* the U.S. has learned how to incorporate the referent object—moderate Islam—into its foreign security policy by dealing with state allies directly instead of with nonstate actors. Unlike the cases of Britain and France, U.S. securitization of religion at the international level of analysis seems to have been more successful because the U.S., operating internationally, has reliable allies that can provide cover for its involvement in the religious sphere and help absorb any blowback or criticism. In short, U.S. involvement in religion abroad is backed up by other's state power. The referent *moderate Islam* has proven a convenient tool to help the U.S. leverage connections in more traditional security sectors such as the military and defense establishments in countries like Indonesia, Philippines, Jordan, and Kuwait. The U.S. continues to expand its securitization of religion in the military and defense sectors even as President Barack Obama attempts to shift U.S. discourse on Islam and religion. The future of U.S. engagement with religion overseas is yet to be determined, however. As of this writing, the U.S. military and defense establishment remains way out in front of the traditional diplomatic (State Department) or development sectors (such as USAID) when it comes to engaging religion abroad for the purposes of national security (Farr 2011). As in Britain and France, those voices calling loudest for greater engagement with religion as a matter of national security put secularists on the defensive.

U.S. ENGAGEMENT WITH RELIGION PRIOR TO 9/11

A handful of scholars in the U.S. began to take note of religion's growing role in international affairs following the end of the Cold War (Rudolph and Piscatori 1997; Casanova 1994; Johnston and Sampson 1995; Huntington 1993). It seemed that religion had indeed been the "missing dimension" of statecraft (Johnston and Sampson 1995). By the late 1990s, President Bill Clinton signed into law the International Religious Freedom Act, which made promoting religious freedom abroad part of U.S. foreign policy, but the U.S. had no overall strategy to engage religious actors and ideas abroad, especially in Muslim majority countries. As former Deputy Assistant Secretary of State Ronald Neumann explained in 1998, "let me be clear and emphatic: the United States of America does not and should not have a political policy toward Islam . . . in our decision-making, religion is not a factor" (quoted in Satloff 2000, 8). Indeed, from 1992 to 1999 the U.S. had well-developed foreign policies towards states and international institutions, "but not religions" (9).

All of this changed after September 11, 2001. After 9/11, the State Department, the Department of Defense, the National Security Council, the CIA, USAID, the National Defense University, the Naval War College, and a number of well-known think tanks explored a range of ways to understand, engage, and influence Muslim populations and the development of Islam in the name of national and international security. U.S. think tanks from across the ideological spectrum were particularly taken with the idea of promoting moderate Muslim voices. Some, like the Rand Corporation, took an especially aggressive approach. A 2003 document entitled *Civil Democratic Islam: Partners, Resources, and Strategies,* speaks of the importance of encouraging Islam's "evolution" (Benard 2003, iii). To encourage a reformation within Islam alliances need to be formed with willing partners, and so the task for policymakers is to "consider very carefully which elements, trends, and forces within Islam they intend to strengthen" (x). The document goes on to offer a typology of Islamic movements, ranging from least to most amenable to U.S. influence and a menu of strategies for how to manipulate each of them. For example, the document notes that "radical fundamentalism . . . tends to alienate large segments of the population with the oppressiveness and rigidity of its approach. We should position ourselves to enhance that alienation" (26). By virtue of their increased alienation from radical Islam, Muslims will come to want what the U.S. wants them to want and thus "find modernism and secularism attractive" (26). Other strategies include encouraging disagreements between traditionalists and fundamentalists while also strengthening the power of traditionalists who may need to be convinced to abandon their "folk Islam" and be "educated and trained in Orthodox Islam" so they can "stand their ground" against the fundamentalists (xi). According to the author, the purpose of all of this is to "help break the fundamentalist, traditionalist monopoly on defining, explaining, and interpreting Islam" (48). Thus the question is not *whether* to intervene in Islam, but who to work with and how to do it. A variety of soft power strategies are offered, such as crafting new textbooks and curricula, working through civic and cultural institutions, and leaning on a variety of media outlets to sow fissure and division within Islam in order to bring radical Muslims around to secularism, democracy, and modernity. The enterprise is of course a risky one, with ample potential for misperception, rejection, and backlash. Acknowledging the challenges ahead the author writes, "it is no easy matter to transform a major world religion. If 'nation-building' is a daunting task, 'religion-building' is immeasurably more perilous and complex" (3).

The Rand Corporation report may seem radically interventionist, but what it envisioned was not far off from what the U.S. was actually doing. By 2005, one reporter wrote an extended expose that concluded, "from military psychological-operations teams and CIA covert operatives to openly funded media and think tanks, Washington is plowing tens of millions of dollars into a campaign to influence not only Muslim societies but Islam itself" (Kaplan 2005, 1). One of the pillars of this effort to influence Islam came in the form of public diplomacy. Public diplomacy essentially refers how countries market themselves. Public diplomacy can range from information or media campaigns to face-to-face meetings or people-to-people connections such as educational exchange programs. The purpose is to gauge foreign perceptions of the U.S. and, when necessary, change them. As Joseph Nye writes, "soft power" refers to "getting others to want what you want" without having to use the coercive threats of economic or military punishment (Nye 2002, 9; Nye 2005). When others come to want what you want, they will acquiesce to your power and, in the best-case scenario, seek to imitate you (Nye 2002, 9). Similarly, U.S. public diplomacy initiatives launched in the wake of 9/11 were meant to improve the perception of the United States, emphasize shared values such as democracy and freedom, and encourage the development of moderate Islam. Initial efforts to engage the Muslim world through public diplomacy were marred by a host of problems, as the United States' "once-powerful arsenal of soft power tools lay neglected since the end of the Cold War" (Kaplan 2005). Early efforts were disorganized and hampered by lack of coordination, leadership, and funding from the executive branch. Bureaucratic infighting and turf wars also took their toll. Eventually, however, U.S. government efforts to engage with Muslim communities overseas received more funding and merged into an interagency program called Muslim World Outreach. Muslim World Outreach went far beyond traditional public diplomacy and reflected the more interventionist approach to religion recommended by think tanks like Rand, the Heritage Foundation, and the Nixon Center.

Muslim World Outreach was launched in 2002 by the National Security Council's Strategic Communication Policy Coordinating Committee. The idea behind this initiative was to encourage the promotion of Western values such as toleration, democracy, peace, and women's rights in Islam through the channels of public diplomacy while encouraging splits between moderate and extremist Muslims. The program was founded on the idea that "the United States and its allies have a national security interest not only in what happens in the Islamic world but within Islam" (Kaplan 2005, 6). Key to the strategy was forging alliances with receptive states and nongovernmental organizations to support versions of Islam that seemed palatable. The U.S. increased funding think tanks such as the Center for Islam and Democracy and the Asia Foundation to support moderate interpretations of the Koran abroad and "foster a body of scholarly research showing liberal Islam's compatibility with democracy and human rights" (8).

The U.S. also encouraged some governments in the Middle East and central Asia (such as Pakistan and Uzbekistan) to promote a renaissance of Sufism (Eteraz 2009). This was based on the assumption that Sufism would make a perfect ally in the War on Terror due to its spiritual, peaceful orientation to the world and its history of political quietism. With Bernard Lewis as its keynote speaker, the Nixon Center in Washington, D.C. even held a conference in 2004 titled "Understanding Sufism and its Potential Role in U.S. Policy" to "explore how Sufism—the spiritual tradition within Islam—relates to U.S foreign policy goals" (Baran 2004). The Heritage Foundation and the Rand Corporation also trumpeted Sufism's history of moderation, arguing that Sufism was a perfect ideological ally for the U.S. government abroad. One scholar even complained that "it is astounding how . . . the U.S. has failed to exploit the massive ideological divisions that separate Sufi Islam from the intolerant puritanical traditions of the Wahhabists" (Jenkins 2004, 27). By 2005, efforts to inform, engage, and influence Arab public opinion and encourage an Islamic reformation had spread to at least 24 countries around the world (Kaplan 2005).

Muslim World Outreach proved controversial. The program seemed to threaten the country's secular traditions, and many in the U.S. diplomatic community expressed reservations that such efforts violated the U.S. constitutional separation between church and state. Moreover, it was dangerous for the U.S. to promote moderate Islam directly to civil society, bypassing the state. On a 2006 visit to Qatar, then Undersecretary of State for Public Diplomacy and Public Affairs Karen Hughes was told by Sheikha Moza, wife of the emir of Qatar and chairperson of the Qatar Foundation, that

"whatever you do will be stamped with the American label and will be re-
jected. Be careful" (Untermeyer 2006). The same year, a U.S. Government
Accountability Office report found that many U.S. soft power efforts during
this period, including Muslim World Outreach, were dismissed outright by
Arab governments as yet another form of U.S. intervention and manipula-
tion into their internal affairs. Governments of "several countries," including
Lebanon and Egypt, refused for "political and other reasons" to broadcast
"Shared Values" videos, which sought to convince Muslim populations that
the United States is not at war with Islam and that Islam and the U.S. shared
the same core values (U.S. Government Accountability Office 2006, 11).
When the State Department conducted its own analysis of the Shared Values
Campaign, it too found that governments and media outlets in many target
countries "found the campaign to be propaganda and unlikely to succeed as
long as U.S. foreign policy remained unchanged" (12).

As its public diplomacy efforts faltered, the Bush administration was
plagued by a host of other problems related to religion that further undermined U.S. efforts to engage and influence Islam abroad. Rumors of the
Koran being flushed down toilets, systematic use of interrogation techniques
specifically designed to exploit detainees' Muslim values and identity, and
the discovery of biblical passages on Pentagon briefing papers and carved
into American weapons—just to name a few examples—further confounded
administration efforts to defuse the suspicion that Islam itself was the target
of the United States' global application of hard power, undermining the
legitimacy of direct outreach efforts to Muslim communities abroad.

Meanwhile, just as Muslim World Outreach struggled to overcome a
host of problems, the U.S. began to increase its engagement with Islam in
more traditional security sectors such as the military and the defense establishment, and found more success when it did so. This occurred most often
when the U.S. military brought religion into its partnerships overseas. As in
all the cases of securitization of religion examined in this book, at the core of
this new military initiative lay the construction of moderate Islam as a referent object for security. The Philippines and Indonesia provide important
test cases of why securitization of religion internationally by the U.S. has
met with some success. In both cases, the construction of moderate Islam
was central to U.S. military and defense partnerships with foreign allies.
This engagement with religion from a distance allows the U.S. to depend
on loyal allies to take the lead in engaging with religion as a dimension of
counter-terrorism, saving the U.S. from having to respond to any resistance
or backlash. In part due to the success of these efforts, the U.S. military has

increased its engagement with religious ideas and actors under the rubric of *smart power.* The securitization of religion by the U.S. is increasing today, with uncertain consequences for the future of U.S. national security.

U.S. NATIONAL SECURITY AND MODERATE ISLAM OVERSEAS

As U.S. public diplomacy efforts launched in the wake of 9/11 struggled to maintain an aura of legitimacy abroad, the U.S. defense and military establishment began to leverage the concept of moderate Islam to shore up security partnerships overseas in the War on Terror. This was particularly evident in Asia. For the U.S. government, Asia was just as important a theater for the War on Terror as the Middle East, and so it became imperative to develop sustainable counter-terrorism alliances with military and defense establishments in the region. Encouraging the promotion of moderate Islam as a counterterrorism strategy was one way to do this. A good example is the Philippines, where the U.S. successfully used the promotion of moderate Islam as a way to develop closer ties to the Philippine military for counter-terrorism and security purposes. It falls to the Philippine government and armed forces, however, not to the U.S., to take the brunt of any resistance to this international securitization of religion.

After 9/11, the U.S. grew concerned over Al Qaeda's global links. In Asia, the group had developed ties to the Abu Sayyaf group, based in the Sulu Archipelago. In 2002 Philippine President Gloria Arroyo and George W. Bush agreed that the U.S. military would be deployed to the Philippines to train the Philippine army to fight Abu Sayyaf, as well as other militant Islamic groups such as the Jemaah Islamiya (Lum 2012, 15). In 2002 alone, the U.S. committed over a thousand troops to the Philippines and gave some $93 million in military aid to the Philippine armed forces to help defeat Abu Sayyaf and related groups as part of Operation Balakitan (Niksch 2007). From then on, U.S. counterterrorism strategy in the country would be handled through U.S. Joint Special Operations Task Force Philippines. "The battle in the Philippines is a battle against an idea," wrote William Eckert, the Command Sergeant Major of JSOTF-Philippines, "and it is being waged by the Joint Special Operations Task Force Philippines" (Eckert 2006, 18). The task force would work closely to increase interoperability with the Philippine army and support other U.S. government programs promoting moderate Islam. Support for moderate Islam was particularly important to help the

Philippine government secure a peace agreement with the Moro Islamic Liberation Front (MILF), a main Islamic separatist group in the Philippines. Promoting the development of moderate Islam in the country contributed to the overall counterterrorism effort by helping to drive a wedge between the MILF and the Jemaah Islamiya and Abu Sayyaf groups.

By January 2005, however, the U.S. was growing impatient with the level of Philippine cooperation. In 2005 U.S. Pacific Command arrived in Manila to place some pressure on the Philippine government to be more aggressive in counterterrorism (Ricciardone 2005). The pressure made the Philippine government very nervous. The Philippines was a challenging country in which to aggressively pursue any religious dimension to the War on Terror given the sensitive nature of the longstanding peace negotiations between the government and a variety of Islamic groups. In this context the promotion of moderate Islam as an aspect of counterterrorism would indeed be a delicate affair. A senior military advisor to Philippine Secretary of Defense Daniel Cruz expressed concern that increased partnership between the U.S. on counterterrorism issues could even endanger the peace process between the Philippine government and the MILF. If the MILF were seen to cooperate with the Philippine government on counterterrorist programs, the official explained, this would only fuel the perception among more radical Islamist groups such as the Jemaah Islamiyah that the MILF's embrace of moderate Islam represented a sellout to the government. Philippine concerns had historical foundations as well, for it was precisely against U.S. military presence in the country that the Moro people of the southern Philippines launched their 10-year rebellion in 1903. According to Cruz's advisor, given the historic tension between the Moro and the Philippine government and the Philippines and the U.S., it was all the more important to conduct the War on Terror in a way that could "ensure there is no big backlash" (Ricciardone 2005).

Still dissatisfied with the level of cooperation and eager to solidify this alliance for the War on Terror, U.S. officials returned to the Philippines in March 2005. Promotion of moderate Islam in the country was high on the agenda, as one U.S. embassy official would later write, because "nurturing "credible voices" of moderate Islam "helps us achieve our counter-terrorism and other policy goals" (Kenney 2008). If the U.S. government and the government of the Philippines could work together on counterterrorism operations and shore up credible voices of moderate Islam, it was argued, the peace process could be furthered and both countries would be more secure. Happily for U.S. officials, things seemed to be moving in the right direction during the second visit of 2005. There seemed to be a change in the attitude of the Philippine armed forces, no doubt due to the February 2005 bombings in Manila and Mindanao by Abu Sayyaf. The simultaneous bombings killed 16, and additional plots were uncovered against other targets in Manila, including the U.S. embassy. Suddenly, the armed forces of the Philippines seemed willing to cooperate, and both sides could agree that "terrorism is arguably more dangerous in the long-term in the Philippines than anywhere in East Asia" (Mussomeli 2005). As events unfolded, the U.S. staff noted that religion seemed to be playing more and more of a significant role in the deterioration of the security situation in the country. While earlier episodes of Islamic extremism in the Philippines were "generally a response to local undertakings, the latest bombing attacks now appear to be religious-inspired—a seeming realization of a long term agenda with religion becoming a central issue behind terrorist acts" (Ricciardone 2005b). Indeed, by 2005 there had been a marked increase in links between Muslim separatist groups in Asia and others in the Middle East, Afghanistan, and Pakistan (Vaughn 2005, 3).

The more religion played a prominent role in the recent increase in violent attacks in the Philippines, the more the U.S began to push the Philippine government to cooperate more on promoting moderate Islam in the country. Among the solutions the embassy recommended were that the Philippine government "support and supervise the teaching of the Arabic language because this is their gateway to a deeper, more moderate understanding of the Koran" (Ricciardone 2005b). The U.S. also launched a $400,000 Madrasah teacher-training project to train 28 Madrasah educators in U.S. values (Ricciardone 2005c). According to the plan, the teachers would travel to the US on a study tour, the purpose being to bring the country's "Islamic educational system into the mainstream."

Despite broad agreement on the general problem, the Philippine government remained exceedingly nervous about being seen to coordinate too closely with the U.S. government on security-related matters, especially those involving religion. Reluctance on the part of the Philippine government was so pronounced that officials from both sides sat down to draw up a continuum of activities that would be "legal," "borderline," or outright "test the limits" of close cooperation (Ricciardone 2005d). So concerned was the Philippine government that the country's Department of National Defense Undersecretary for Policy Antonio Santos suggested that an "information campaign" be developed to educate the Philippine public on U.S. government counterterrorism support for the Philippines (Ricciardone 2005d).

The U.S. ambassador chalked up such reluctance to "misplaced nationalist sentiment" (Ricciardone 2005d).

Nonetheless, the U.S. government engaged in some positive reinforcement, applauding Philippine progress in grappling with the "existential challenges to Philippine democracy and security" (Ricciardone 2005b). But things were not improving. Close cooperation between the U.S. and Philippine military was making life very difficult for the Philippine government, and it was they who bore the brunt of domestic backlash against the counter terrorism projects and engagement with religious actors. Norberto Gonzales, the national security advisor of the Philippines, provided the U.S. ambassador with a report about Islamic extremism in his country in the spring of 2005. In it he reported that "Islamist extremism in the Philippines was no longer a reaction to domestic events and policies, but rather against so-called 'Muslim infidels' and the powers and nations that support the latter, i.e., the U.S. and, by extension, the Philippines" (Ricciardone 2005b). U.S. embassy staff had to concur in its gloss on Gonzales's report, noting that the conflicts in the Philippines were "not between two religions," but rather "proxies to [sic] a global war internal to the Muslims against so-called 'Muslim infidels' and the powers and nations that support the latter" (Ricciardone 2005b). The U.S. Ambassador wrote in conclusion that "the Philippines has become a target of these terrorist agenda [sic] because it is known as a loyal ally of the United States" (Ricciardone 2005b).

As time went on, the U.S continued its engagement in the country, helping the Philippine government to back moderates among the MILF and others such as the Ulema Forum for Peace and Democracy in order to isolate "radical elements" within the group and support the peace process between the group and the government. In 2006 the U.S. deputy chief of mission in Manila expressed the need to "think innovatively and creatively about how to introduce moderate Muslim role models in Mindanao" (Jones 2006). By 2008 U.S. Ambassador Kristi Kenney reported that the embassy's "top Mission strategic goal is to promote peace and counter violent extremism throughout the country" by nurturing "credible voices" to "help us achieve our counter-terrorism and other policy goals" (Kenney 2008). The correspondence went on to emphasize that as the U.S. cultivated its relationship with the Philippine government and continued it counterterrorism work "it is important to their continued credibility that they not be perceived to be speaking on our behalf or at our behest" (Kenney 2008).

Following 9/11, the U.S. defense and military establishments seemed to have been able to help the Philippine government in its peace negotiations with the MILF by promoting moderate interpretations of Islam as a way to shore up relations between moderate elements of the MILF and the government. Indeed, considering the decade-long involvement in the Philippines from 2001 to 2011, about 60 percent of U.S. aid to the country went to programs to "mitigate the economic and political conditions that make extremist ideologies and activities attractive," especially in Mindanao and the Sulu Archipelago (Lum 2012, 1). Such programs were designed to increase the credibility of the armed forces of the Philippines and simultaneously demonstrate to groups such as Abu Sayyaf, the MILF, and the JI that "there are benefits to working with the AFP" and turning away from violent extremism (Lum 2012, 1; Kenney 2008). Such a success in the development of moderate Islam in the Philippines has come at a cost, however, as the Philippine government itself has become a target of terror precisely because of its cooperation with the U.S. Nonetheless, through its promotion of moderate Islam and its engagement with religion, the U.S. able to help further the peace negotiations between the Moro Islamic Liberation Front and the Philippine government while solidifying its military and counterterrorism alliance with the Philippines.

Indonesia

A similar dynamic took place in Indonesia, where the U.S. encourages the development of moderate Islam as a way to shore up and expand a bilateral U.S.-Indonesian alliance. In early 2006, U.S. Secretary of State Condoleezza Rice travelled to Jakarta to begin a new security partnership with the country. The U.S. expected Indonesia to play a greater role in regional security issues and the War on Terror, and in return, pledged its support for democratic reform. Indeed, the U.S. had a great stake in seeing democracy come to fruition in Indonesia, the largest Muslim country in the world. For the United States, the building of a modern, moderate Islam in Indonesia was a crucial national security objective, as Indonesia's position as the largest Muslim nation and an up and coming democracy made it a major player in the global struggle between "democratic modernization and militant retrograde Islam" (Amselem 2006). For the U.S., Indonesia was an ideological battleground and winning the war of ideas there was central to U.S. national security. As the *Washington Post* reported from Jakarta, "today, Indonesia is a democracy and the role of Islam is one of the most important issues facing U.S. policy in the country . . . what kind of Islam prevails here is critical to U.S. interests across the wider Muslim world" (Higgins 2009).

The U.S. began to promote certain interpretations of Islam over others in Indonesia immediately after 9/11, as "hundreds of Indonesian clerics went through U.S.-sponsored courses that taught a reform-minded reading of the Koran. A handbook for preachers, published with U.S. money, offered tips on what to preach. One American-funded group even tried to script Friday prayer sermons" (Higgins 2009). Through such programs and initiatives the U.S. assisted the Indonesian government to amplify the voices of moderate Islam in order to win the global war of religious ideas. The promotion of moderate Islam also helped Indonesia to move away from nonaligned attitudes of the past and "act as a moderating, democratic influence on more radical regimes in the Middle East" (Amselem 2006).

Together, the U.S. and Indonesian governments embarked on a number of programs designed to retrain terrorists in moderate Islam and enlist reformed individuals for intelligence collection and further deradicalization efforts. The U.S. embassy cofunded workshops to explore such deradicalization initiatives and help remove the underlying ideology that supports terrorism. U.S. Ambassador Cameron Hume reported how in Indonesia "we use our assistance, exchange, and outreach programs to assist moderate mainstream groups spread their message of tolerance, which reinforces our interests and serves to spread our message" (Hume 2008c). Indonesia indeed offered a unique opportunity for the U.S. to work with a foreign state to find moderate Muslim allies to help win the war within Islam. With over 70 million members between them, moderate Muslim organizations in Indonesia such as the Nahdlatul Ulema and the Muhammadiya represented, in the eyes of the U.S., the most important allies in the fight against radical religious ideas.

The U.S. and Indonesian governments were able to report some tangible successes in their joint efforts to promote moderate Islam. One of Indonesia's two main Muslim representative organizations, the Nahdlatul Ulema (NU), issued a statement in 2007 condemning the idea that Indonesian Muslims should work toward turning the country into an Islamic caliphate. In a 2007 meeting with the U.S. embassy, a "high level NU official" reported that although the statement had come from the NU's East Java chapter, the NU as a whole was moving toward supporting it (Hume 2007). The NU official made it clear in additional meetings with the U.S. embassy staff that the organization was locked in a heated theological battle with other Indonesian

Muslim organizations that were pushing their own interpretations of Islam. In a meeting with one of the NU's rival groups, the Muhammadiya, the U.S. responded that it "has no interest in getting involved in theology, but given that many extremists supported the Caliphate idea it seemed appropriate to take them head-on and underscore support for a sovereign state that guarantees religious freedom" (Hume 2007). The U.S. had few qualms about backing some Muslim groups over others if doing so could help to shore up the post–9/11 U.S.-Indonesian alliance. Promoting moderate Islam was also in Indonesia's interest. As Dewi Fortuna Anwar, a foreign affairs advisor to Indonesia's vice president remarked, "before 9/11 Islam was not seen as an asset in Indonesian foreign policy, but after the events Indonesia's moderate Muslim identity, its thriving democracy and economic openness . . . fused into a total package in its foreign policy" (Gnietwotta and Ririhena 2011). By 2010, Indonesia's President Yudhoyno had begun to deliberately translate Indonesia's model of moderate, democratic Islam into an increasingly active foreign policy in the region.

The U.S. had to remain behind the scenes in Indonesia despite its success in using moderate Islam as an ideological lever to solidify its partnership with the new Indonesian government. Hume was quite aware of this. "It is far better to have Indonesian Muslim groups articulate and demonstrate the benefits of peace, prosperity and tolerance than for us to talk about it," he wrote in 2008 (Hume 2008b). "We have found it more effective when these messages are disseminated as independent Indonesian or official GOI [*sic*] views rather than appearing to originate from the U.S. government" (Hume 2008c). On the Indonesian side, the government's chief counterterrorism coordinator agreed, underscoring "the negative impact if the general public learned of U.S. sponsorship" of programs to promote moderate Islam (Hume 2008a). Both intuitions proved correct. In 2006, a hardline Indonesian Islamist magazine had criticized the Asia Foundation as a CIA front organization trying to "change the face of Islam." The Asia Foundation had indeed "took the lead in battling noxious strands of Islam in Indonesia as part of a USAID-funded program called Islam and Civil Society" (Higgins 2009).

In the Philippines and Indonesia, the U.S. was able to shore up counterterrorism cooperation and reinforce bilateral alliances by working with both governments to promote moderate Islam. But U.S. had to do so at a distance. It is because of this behind-the-scenes approach that the securitization of religion has managed to avoid some of the problems experienced by Britain and France at the domestic level of analysis. For one thing, the promotion of moderate Islam overseas by the U.S. is not tied to the development of particular, national identity as was the case in Britain and France. The development of moderate Islam in the Philippines or Indonesia, though crucial for U.S. national security according to U.S. policymakers, does not depend for its success on the formation of an American version of Islam or even on agreement with U.S. foreign policy. Instead, what the U.S. is most concerned with in its international securitization of religion is bringing into being a moderate version of Islam that will help improve counterterrorism and diplomatic and military ties in strategically important regions such as Asia. The securitization of religion is in such cases a means to an end. As long as the U.S. remains steps removed from the process of developing moderate Islam, it is able to use religion as a tool to promote national security, leaving the intelligence and security forces of the partnering country to manage any resistance or countermovements. For both the Philippines and Indonesia, the rise of moderate Islam with outside support but minimal explicit involvement helps each country to drive ideological wedges in between different Islamist groups and also to move into a more favorable geopolitical position in their region.

Securitization of Religion in the U.S. Military

Unfortunately for the Bush administration, the successes the U.S. experienced in promoting moderate Islam in Asia were overshadowed by the fact that the War on Terror was not going well. As mentioned previously, a succession of events undermined at every turn the administration's claim that the U.S. respected Muslims and the religion of Islam and did not intend to direct its coercive power against the Muslim world as a whole. Rumors continued to circulate of U.S. soldiers desecrating the Koran in Bagram prison in Afghanistan, in Iraq, in Guantanamo Bay, in CIA black sites, and elsewhere. The 2004 release of photos of Iraqi prisoners subject to torture and cruel, inhuman, and degrading punishment at the hands of their U.S. guards made matters even worse. Danish cartoons depicting the Prophet Muhammad as a terrorist appeared in 2005 and led to worldwide protests. The combined impact of these events, one after the other, reinforced the perception that proclamations to the contrary, the U.S. and its allies were in fact at war with Islam and sought to punish all Muslims for what happened on 9/11.

When Barack Obama took office in early 2009, he immediately set out to improve relations with Muslim communities around the world. In well-publicized speeches in Cairo and Ankara Obama attempted to set U.S. relations with the Muslim world—Muslims both at home and abroad—on a new course by reiterating that the U.S. was not in fact at war with Islam. Obama reassured audiences that U.S. engagement with Islam would no longer be based exclusively on national security concerns. As Obama remarked in his speech in Ankara, "America's relationship with the Muslim community and the Muslim world cannot and will not just be based upon opposition to terrorism" (Obama 2009). To prove the point, Obama instated a "whole of government" engagement with Islam, tasking even NASA with outreach to Muslim communities abroad (York 2010). One detects a rolling of the eyes when NASA administrator Charles Bolden remarked that "he wanted me to find a way to reach out to the Muslim world . . . to help them feel good about their historic contribution to science" (York 2010).

Meanwhile in the diplomatic establishment, the Obama administration created a new position in the State Department, a Special Representative to Muslim Communities. As of this writing the post is occupied by Farah Pandith, an Indian-born Muslim American with prior experience at the State Department, USAID, and the National Security Council. When interviewed for this book Pandith remarked that the purpose of her position is to "build new networks for . . . new narratives that are coming up" among Muslim youth around the globe. According to Pandith, "we are using the strength of the United States government to be the convener and the facilitator and the intellectual partner for the ideas we hear on the ground and move them forward" (Pandith 2011).

After tasking U.S. agencies with outreach to Muslim communities and improving diplomatic outreach to the Muslim world, Obama moved on to sever the connection between religion and Islam in U.S. national security discourse. All references to jihad, Islam, the war of ideas, and Islamic extremism were removed from the national security strategy of the U.S. The 2010 National Security Strategy included none of these terms or phrases. Such language, the administration argued, only gives "credence to the lie" that "the U.S. is at war with Islam" and further alienates moderate Muslims abroad (Scarborough 2010).

As with the Bush administration, however, events continued to frustrate the Obama administration's efforts to control the message on religion and national security. The extended protests in New York City against the construction of a mosque near Ground Zero and, at the same time, threats made by a Florida pastor to publicly burn copies of the Koran further reinforced the perception around the world that beneath the ongoing War on Terror lay a deep-seated American fear and hostility toward Islam and Muslims. The Obama administration was so concerned that the combined force of the two events would undermine the very narrative it worked so hard to cultivate that the Department of Defense intervened, calling on the Florida pastor not to go through with the planned International Burn a Koran Day. Though Burn a Koran Day did not take place, protests were held worldwide and many were killed or wounded in India, Pakistan, Afghanistan, Kashmir, Iran, Gaza, Indonesia, and elsewhere. Indeed, in the sensitive post–9/11 environment, anything and everything having to do with the United States' relationship to Islam, no matter how obscure or outlandish, elevated automatically to a matter of national security (Bosco and Hartman-Mahmud 2012). While Obama changed official U.S. discourse about religion and Islam in the State Department, the White House, and in the National Security Strategy, the U.S. defense and military establishments incorporated religion more and more into their strategic thinking and battlefield operations. In fact, drawing on successes in places like the Philippines and Indonesia, the U.S. securitization of religion abroad increased. The military and defense establishments took the lead in this effort, reinforced and encouraged by the U.S. think-tank community.

In Britain, the state based its engagement with religious ideas and actors on the conviction that national security is best achieved through strengthening community cohesion. In France, Sarkozy sought closer ties with Muslim representative organizations in the wake of 9/11 and justified the attempt by appeal to positive *laicite*. Like Britain and France, the U.S., too, has developed its own leitmotif for closer engagement with religion. In U.S foreign policy, defense, and think-tank circles, this is known as "smart power." There are different versions of what smart power precisely refers to. According to the Center for Strategic and International Studies, smart power seems to refer to what is known in International Relations jargon as hegemonic stability theory: "providing things people and governments in all quarters of the world want but cannot attain in the absence of American leadership" (CSIS 2007, 1). That is, smart power refers to the U.S. as the specially ordained provider of global public goods.

To the U.S. public, however, it was General David Petraeus, the "scholar-warrior," who helped to popularize the concept of smart power (Entous and Stewart 2010). In Petreaus's version, smart power involves leading others to see that, contrary to their own intuitions, they share the same values and want the same things as the United States. Smart power should be able to succeed in changing the perceptions that others may have of the U.S. and its intentions. Smart power is not meant to replace hard power, which refers to the use of coercion—killing. Rather, smart power refers to getting others to accept that the exercise of American hard power is necessary, legitimate, and in everyone's interest. As the War on Terror began to accumulate an impressive list of failures to match its successes, smart power became something of a corrective buzz word in U.S. academic, think tank, and policy circles. By the time the Obama administration took office, smart power would, according to Petraeus, become the new guiding philosophy of the U.S. military and diplomatic establishment.

In September 2009, Petraeus signed the Joint Unconventional Warfare Taskforce Executive Order to expand clandestine operations in countries throughout the Middle East, central Asia, Asia, and the Horn of Africa. Petraeus's directive signified a massive international expansion of U.S. covert operations and exemplified the new equation: that soft power plus hard power equals smart power. In the directive, Petraeus argued that information gathered from all over the globe would give not only troops but also foreign businessmen, academics, and others in the soft power realm "persistent situational awareness" of the global battlefield of the War on Terror (Mazzetti 2010).

As it turned out, religion is a crucial ingredient of situational awareness and has a central role to play in the new ideology of smart power. U.S. military publications give a unique insight into how the armed forces undertake quite seriously to incorporate religion into strategic planning and battlefield operations. Take the *U.S. Army Stability Operations Field Manual,* for example. The manual points out that "during stability operations, leaders and Soldiers become governors in a much broader sense, influencing events and circumstances normally outside the bounds of the military instrument of national power" (United States Army 2008, 5-48). Thus "the burdens of governance upon a transnational military authority require culturally astute leaders and Soldiers capable of adapting to nuances of religion" (5-48). Under such conditions it is necessary that the new generation of scholar-warriors recognize "the depth to which religious and political factors interact in other societies drives the motivations and perceptions of the local populace" (5-49). As in Britain, where security forces, intelligence gatherers, and local police were urged to "get a grip on faith," U.S. military and intelligence personnel would also do well to appreciate how profoundly religion shapes the perceptions and motivations of the subject population.

Incorporating religion into military strategic thinking is not just a theoretical exercise. In a 2006 issue of *Special Warfare,* the technical journal of the army's JFK Special Warfare Center and School in Fort Bragg, North Carolina, Chaplain (Major) Timothy K. Bedsole details how U.S. Army Special Operations forces are learning to incorporate religion into their operations through the prism of cultural intelligence, a key component of smart power. The article details how religion is included in battlefield and strategic planning calculations through something called "religious factors analysis" or RFA. According to Bedsole, "there is a need to integrate a new religious-factors analysis, or RFA, into the intelligence preparation of the battlefield (IPB) process so that religious factors become actionable elements of the mission plan" (Bedsole 2006, 9).

Knowledge of RFAs is very important for, among other things, predicting how a community will respond to the presence of U.S. Special Forces. In order to know this, Special Forces must take an active role in learning about religion at the local level. According to Bedsole:

> If we fail to consider the dynamics of religion in a culture, we limit our intelligence and allow religion to remain a secret code of motivating messages and symbols that will confound our analysis and hamper our understanding of the enemy's center of gravity. (2006, 10)

Knowing religion will thus make the intentions and plans of insurgents more transparent by allowing forces to read and interpret secret enemy symbols, signals, and codes. A particularly interesting feature of the passage quoted above is the concept of the "enemy's center of gravity." The "center of gravity" refers in fact to the majority of citizens who could go either way with their loyalties or who seek to remain neutral. The major argues, in effect, that knowledge of religion will help Special Operations Forces not only to gather intelligence from a community without offending them—ensuring future cooperation—but also tip the loyalty of the population in the allies' favor. The assumption seems to be that subject populations are more willing to give up intelligence to outside forces that have made an effort to understand them. However one puts it, according to Bledsoe the ultimate goal is to win the war on terror by defeating the "exploitation of religion for political and ideological purposes" that is a hallmark not of the U.S. military, but of the enemy (10). Here, as in the *U.S. Army Field Manual,* religion is presented as an aspect of the battlefield terrain, much like geographical features or the position of enemy forces. One must consider, among other things, important local religious leaders, what ideas typically encourage violence, what memories, myths, or narratives exist that define the identity of the local community, religious sites, their location, symbolism, and use by the local population, and much more. All of these are necessary because "understanding the way that religious ideology shapes the greater society and individuals can provide the commander with the greatest ability to shape the battlefield of the hearts and minds" (14).

The following year, another article appeared in the same journal discussing the importance of religious factor analysis, but here the authors are more blunt (Courter, Fiegle, and Shofner 2007). They argue that sensitivity to religion or identifying key religious players or beliefs is not enough. Rather, it is more important to discover how religion motivates the behaviors, influences the perceptions, and conditions the reactions of the target population. Religious knowledge is important to help predict what is termed "potential populace behavior" (Courter, Fiegle, and Shofner 2007, 26). Specifically, studying the religious beliefs and customs of the community can expose fault lines—theological, political, or cultural differences between and among groups—that, owing to their sensitivity, can be exploited by the command for intelligence gathering or to sway loyalties. An added benefit of cultivating an in-depth understanding of the religious beliefs and customs of a population is that such knowledge is particularly valuable when deciding how to tailor psychological operations, or "PSYOPs," to a particular target audience in order to shape their behavior and influence their perceptions and reactions. Cultivating loyal allies—religious figures willing to share information—is paramount to the overall success of military engagement with religion in the AO, or Area of Operations. This is of course a dangerous game in large part because, as the U.S. Army Counterinsurgency Field Manual points out, potential recruits for insurgent campaigns "often include individuals receptive to the message that the West is dominating their religion through puppet governments and local surrogates" (CSIS 2011). As in the Philippines and Indonesia, the perception that the U.S. is seeking to manipulate or change religious beliefs can be a debilitating obstacle to counter-insurgency or reconstruction operations.

In addition to seeking a greater knowledge of the religion of target populations the U.S. military's securitization of religion overseas also includes encouraging the construction of moderate Islam. There are many examples of this. In 2010 one army company in Afghanistan conceived and executed a program to train Afghan religious leaders dubbed Voices of Moderate Islam. In the words of the U.S. army major who helped conceive and design the program, "we determined that the way to fight radical Islam within the context of an Afghan counter-insurgency was with the true, moderate message of Islam. In short, Islam will police itself" (Yandura 2011, 13). As always, the task force was able to achieve this theostrategic objective with the help of a powerful sovereign ally. In cooperation with Jordanian Special Forces, and under the sponsorship of the U.S. embassies in Kabul, Amman, and the Jordanian Hashemite Charity Organization, the 173rd Airborne Brigade Combat Team—Taskforce Bayonnet—arranged for 35 Afghani Muslim leaders to travel to Jordan for religious education. Upon arrival they were met by and shared a meal with King Abdullah. On the following day the participants experienced the seminar phase of the program, during which the group spent a full day with Egyptian and Jordanian religious figures from the U.S. embassy in Jordan, the Islamic University in Jordan, and the Jordanian armed forces director of Iftar. During the seminars the participants discussed and debated topics such as what is moderate Islam; why it matters; the social, political, and religious duties of Muslims; and who is authorized to issue a fatwa (15). After the instruction in Jordan, the attendees then made the pilgrimage to Mecca. Returning to Afghanistan as respected hajjis, the participants could then use their new legitimacy to "help erode the credibility of a major theme of the insurgent narrative," that the U.S. does not respect Islam, thus winning a key ideological victory over "radical suppressive ideology" (11). No longer, Yandura declared, could the "insurgents" claim that "coalition forces are here to interfere with Islam" (Task Force Bayonet 2010, 2).

The U.S. military also engaged in expanding its methods to promote moderate Islam in Afghanistan, including a reeducation program in moderate Islam for former radicals detained at Bagram Air Force Base (IslamOnline 2009). In Singapore, Malaysia, Indonesia, and Saudi Arabia, security forces have engaged in deprogramming radicals by teaching them moderate Islam, and the U.S. military has sought to imitate such programs and introduced similar religious rehab programs in Iraq (Montlake 2007; Stern 2010). Like Indonesia, Kuwait too seeks to become "a shining center of moderate dogma for the world" and the U.S. diplomatic, military, and defense establishment is helping the country to make it happen, wrote U.S. Ambassador Richard LeBaron (LeBaron 2006b). In 2006 National Security Bureau President Shaykh Sabah Al-Khaled told LeBaron that the government of Kuwait developed a five-year plan to train imams, promote moderation, and assert control over the country's mosques. "It's not on the battlefield that you win," remarked Al-Khaled, "but in the ideas" (LeBaron 2006a). The U.S. military continued to work with the Kuwaiti Security Forces on programs to that "focus on the dangers of misunderstanding religion" and "correcting misunderstandings about the role of Islam in Kuwait and the region" (LeBaron 2005).

Religion and U.S. National Security: A Growing Consensus?

As the U.S. military and defense establishments increasingly incorporate religion into their planning and operations, the U.S. think-tank community provides intellectual support. As always, promoting certain interpretations of Islam over others is a key aspect of the approach. In 2009 the U.S. Institute of Peace launched its Muslim World Initiative to address "the vital foreign policy and national security challenges associated with the many and diverse Islamic societies around the globe" (Solomon 2009, ix). The initiative had three major stated objectives: mobilizing moderate Islamists to garner their support for democracy promotion, marginalizing militants and extremists, and generally "bridging the divide between the United States and the Muslim World" (ix). According to the USIP, Islam is in need of reform and renewal and the United States is specially tasked with leading such a reformation, even if that means taking a more interventionist role in theology

In another example of how U.S. think tanks contribute to the international securitization of religion, the Chicago Council on Global Affairs has produced a wide-ranging and comprehensive statement of the use of smart power to influence Islam in a 2010 report, *Engaging Religious Communities Abroad: A New Imperative for U.S. Foreign Policy* (Chicago Council 2010). The report was written by a team of over 30 academics, religious leaders, members of the U.S. foreign policy community, development agencies, and other nongovernmental organizations. The report "exhorts government and non-governmental actors in the United States" to find ways to "understand and work with religious actors to promote American interests around the world" (Chicago Council 2010, 19). The authors are confident that the United States will be able to achieve this goal while avoiding being seen as manipulating religion, getting entangled in theological debates, or otherwise channeling the discussion in directions favorable to the U.S. strategic and national security agenda. Nonetheless, the report notes that "from a strategic perspective," it is unfortunate that the United States "lacks the standing to influence" interreligious debates that often have an impact on the wider world. For the U.S. has a profound interest in the outcome of these debates, and so, as the U.S. military tried to do in places like Afghanistan, the Philippines, Indonesia, and elsewhere, the strategy is to influence religious ideas and actors indirectly, or, in the words of the authors, "develop the means to assist those whose ideas" the U.S. supports (49). This should help to ensure that those who do form ideological alliances with the United States will not be "regarded by their communities as lackeys" of her (49).

Echoing Petraeus's belief that business and academia have a role to play in the War on Terror, the Chicago Report envisions that the U.S. government "and its partners operating from nongovernmental sectors such as higher education and business—should concentrate on creating a structural environment that will ultimately bring about the desired ends" (51). What are the desired ends? In part, to "greatly reduce the probability that the growth in influence of religious communities will collide with America's interests and values" (51). In order to ensure this outcome the report argues that the National Security Council should be the "guardian" of the United States' religious initiatives and responsible for defining the "strategic parameters of engagement" with religious communities abroad (56).

The general movement of U.S. think tanks to support the connection between increased engagement with religion abroad and national security can also be detected in the shift in discourse around religious freedom. The original 1998 International Religious Freedom Act barely mentions national security at all, aside from a commitment to direct U.S. development and security assistance "to governments other than those found to be engaged in gross violation of the right to freedom of religion" and the creation of an advisor on issues of international religious freedom in the National Security Council (International Religious Freedom Act 1998, 3). After 9/11, however, the promotion of International Religious Freedom abroad is now cast in explicitly security-laden language (Seiple and Hoover 2004; Farr 2008). As William Inboden remarked at a recent conference, "there is a notable correlation between religious freedom and security; one would be hard pressed to find a nation that respects religious freedom and also poses a security threat to the United States" (Berkley Center 2010, 6). Eric Patterson, Assistant Director of the Berkley Center, added, "a wise and prudent American religious liberty policy would begin by operationalizing . . . concrete policy action congruent with U.S. foreign policy and security interests" (8).

In a final example of how U.S. think tanks intellectually underwrite increasing securitization of religion, explicit synergies are evolving between some think tanks and the military. Grant money from well-known foundations such as the Luce Foundation has allowed for a variety of partnerships between scholars of religion, think tanks, and the National Defense University. In December 2010, staff of the Berkley Center for Religion, Peace

& World Affairs led a simulation at the U.S. Naval Academy, called Reconstruction Operations in Highly Religious Societies. The simulation was also run at the U.S. Military Academy, the National Defense University, the Marine Corps University, and the Armed Forces Chaplain Center (Berkley Center 2010–2011). In an interview, codirector of the Berkley Center, Tom Farr, noted that it is indeed true that the U.S. military is "way out in front" of the U.S. diplomatic establishment on bringing religion into its routine operations. As Farr went on to explain:

> qualms about religion tend to dissipate when you have to figure out how to deal with the problem on the ground. And the Petraeus counterinsurgency doctrine is a pretty good example of this; if you've got to hold the ground that you've taken by gaining the loyalty and the friendship of a heavily Muslim village, staying away from religion is the last thing in the world you want to do. (Farr 2011)

Thus the Berkley Center and a number of other U.S. think tanks understand themselves as contributing to overall effort, spearheaded by the military and defense establishment, to bring religion further into the practice of the national security establishment. Promoting religious freedom, incorporating religion into battlefield awareness and strategy, and promoting moderate Islam are cornerstones of these efforts.

It seems that the U.S. military and defense establishment is indeed "way out in front": *too far* in fact, for the diplomatic and development cultures in the U.S. government. Just as in Britain and France, post–9/11 efforts to engage with religion more explicitly strain the familiar boundaries of the secular. In the U.S. State Department, for example, the U.S. Foreign Service remains skeptical, even hesitant, to make closer engagement with religious ideas and actors part of its official portfolio. Perhaps more than any other, Farr has written about the reluctance of the U.S. Foreign Service to train its ambassadors and FSOs in religion in any serious or consistent way. In the 2010 Chicago Council report, the authors were divided among themselves over whether a presidential directive was needed to clarify the Establishment Clause of the U.S. Constitution to allow the U.S. foreign policy establishment to take a more active and explicit role in understanding, engaging, and influencing religious actors abroad. A similar reluctance exists in the U.S. aid and development establishment. While the U.S. military has been given more freedom to "fund Islamic causes" under the rubric of smart power, USAID remains reticent about engaging religion abroad for fear of violating the U.S. establishment clause. The legal test, according to Gary Winter, USAID's legal counsel, is whether USAID activities include "endorsement of a religion, indoctrination of religions," or "excessive entanglement with religion." The agency has to "try to accomplish our secular purpose while still not violating these legal principles" (Lynch 2009).

CONCLUSION

The shape of U.S. securitization of religion abroad is now clear. In contrast to both Britain and France, the U.S. securitized religion internationally in the wake of September 11. For reasons of national security the U.S. diplomatic establishment overseas partnered with its allies to encourage the formation of moderate interpretations of Islam. This was an unprecedented step for a country that until this point had largely confined its activity regarding religion overseas to promoting religious freedom. Following 9/11, however, the U.S. diplomatic and defense establishments increasingly incorporated engagement with religious ideas and actors into the strategy of the global war on terror. While the U.S. encouraged reformation in Islam through many of the same policies that Britain and France did, the United States' reliance on foreign state allies allowed it to largely avoid the backlash and controversy from Muslim communities and civil society that ultimately led to securitization's failure in Britain and France. Promoting moderate Islam abroad also emerged as a useful way for the U.S. to strengthen its bilateral security partnerships with a number of countries such as the Philippines, Indonesia, Jordan, and Kuwait.

The U.S. securitization of religion is increasing overseas, and the military and defense establishments are leading the way. The larger U.S. foreign policy community increasingly converges around the notion that engaging with religious ideas and actors abroad is vital for U.S. strategic interests. This requires the collaboration of the military, defense, diplomatic, and even academic establishments under the rubric of smart power. However, as the U.S. increases its engagement with religious ideas and actors abroad, it struggles anew with its own secular traditions. Thus, as with Britain and France, the securitization of religion brings to the surface deep tensions within secularity.

Conclusion

Religion, "The Smartest Power of All"?

This book has examined how three secular Western states grapple with religion's increasing role in the public sphere. I argued that in the wake of 9/11, all three secular states construct religion, and especially Islam, as a referent object for security. Following the Copenhagen School of security studies, I refer to this general phenomenon as the *securitization of religion* and I have argued that this securitization arises in response to an acute post–9/11 security conundrum: secular, Western states, convinced that an irreducibly religious element lies beneath acts of violent terrorism, can no longer ignore the role of religion in global politics and know they must understand and engage religious ideas and actors but are unsure how. If secular states ignore the role of religion, they discount emerging threats to their security. If on the other hand they engage religious ideas and actors in the public sphere, they risk creating new cycles of insecurity through mistrust, suspicion, and resistance. The purpose of this book is to conceptualize this general security problem, identify the ways three secular Western states try to deal with it, and examine the consequences of their discourses and policies in comparative perspective. Here, I review the findings of this book and then offer some concluding thoughts on three remaining issues: the relationship between the securitization of religion and secularism, the question of the Western secular state and Islam, and the normative implications of the securitization of religion.

As I have argued, the securitization of religion refers to the general process of how secular states engage with religion in a post–9/11 world. A central feature of this process is the construction of moderate Islam as a referent object for security, or something to be protected from threat. By encouraging the development of certain interpretations of Islam over others, Western secular states hope not only to cut the ideological roots of violence but also form durable alliances with religious actors for the purposes of national security. Securitizing religion is partly a matter of framing, as I showed in chapter 2, but it also includes specific policies. Such policies, common to all of the case studies in this book, include training or retraining religious leaders such as imams, forming alliances with Muslim representative organizations or creating new ones, training police and security forces in understanding religion, and encouraging the academy, think tanks, and other points of intellectual production to contribute to this knowledge-intensive effort.

Once the securitization of religion is seen as a whole that consists of both discursive and policy elements, a pattern emerges. In chapter 2 I provided a structured analysis of three elite, post–9/11 discourses on religion and Islam. I showed how the securitization of religion is premised not upon the construction of Islam as a threat in the manner of the clash of civilizations but on precisely the opposite contention: that there is no clash between the West and Islam but rather a war of ideas within Islam itself. The war is between the moderates and the radicals within Islam. Because moderate Islam happens to coincide with a number of secular, liberal Western values, elites argue, Western secular states must takes sides in Islam's internal war and help to win in it in the name of (inter)national security. Chapter 2 thus demonstrated that all three political elites framed the big picture in a similar way, and that this framing underpinned the similar policies that each state took regarding religion in the public sphere. But these discursive and policy similarities led to different outcomes. Aside from the obvious difference that one general phenomenon manifests itself in three different national contexts, securitizations succeed in some cases and fail in others. Thus, having laid out the basics of securitization theory, as well as what is meant by success and failure from that theoretical perspective, I demonstrated in the following empirical chapters that level of analysis—whether the securitization of religion takes place at the domestic or international level—can help explain the different outcomes we see.

Specifically, in both Britain and France, civil society resistance led to securitization's failure. In the case of Britain, I illustrated how Blair's discourse on religion and national security trickled down to lower levels of the British state and traced the development of Britain's Prevent program and its ultimate failures. The state engaged in a variety of concrete policies to promote a moderate interpretation of Islam to strengthen the role of religion in the public sphere as part of secure, cohesive communities. The state encouraged panels, working groups, and Muslim representative organizations such as the Muslim Council of Britain to assist in helping to execute the state's security agenda. It even helped to create new representative organizations when needed, such as the Sufi Muslim Council and others. Moreover, the British state supported the formation of working groups to train imams, established theology boards at leading universities, and trained police and security forces in understanding religion, especially Islam. As time went on, participants became less enamored of the Prevent program as it became clear that the government had securitized religion by promoting certain interpretations over Islam over others and mixing up programs designed to promote moderate Islam with community cohesion and intelligence gathering. In short, as the House of Commons hearings and other responses show, many Muslims in Britain came to feel that the secular British state had turned the interpretation of their faith into a matter of loyalty and political obligation.

A similar process unfolded in France, where state engagement with religion has a long history. As minister of the interior and later as president, Sarkozy encouraged the creation of the country's largest Muslim representative organization, the *Conseil Francais de Culte Musulman* (CFCM), in the wake of 9/11 to help promote a modern, moderate Islam of France, among other duties. The council combined into a single umbrella organization a number of preexisting representative Muslim organizations such as the National Federation of the Muslims of France, the Union of the Islamic Organizations of France, and others. Almost immediately, France's Muslim community fractured over the founding of the CFCM. In 2003 alone, the year the CFCM was founded, four separate Muslim groups sprang up to provide a secular alternative to the CFCM: the *Mouvement des Musulmans Laiques de France*, the *Conseil Francais des Musulmans Laiques*, the *Conseil des Democrates Musulmans de France*, and the *Convention Laique pour l'Egalite des droits* (Cesari 2004). This was a harbinger of the resistance that was to come against Sarkozy's conception of positive *laicite*, according to which the French state must acknowledge its own religious roots, engage more with religion in the public sphere than ever before, and actively promote and even fund the emergence of a moderate, modern Islam of France. According to Sarkozy, France's Muslims communities, and especially the CFCM, were duty bound to support the state's security agenda and encourage the development of moderate Islam. As chapter 4 showed, however, just as in Britain, Muslim communities in France resisted such state intrusion into religious matters, were suspicious of what motives lay behind the officially sanctioned development of an Islam of France, and did not trust the new umbrella organizations designed to promote it. The French security establishment was even forced to concede that the state's attempt to organize Islam was one of the main reasons behind recent terrorist attacks in the country.

In the U.S. case, however, the securitization of religion met a different outcome. Unlike Britain and France, which attempted to encourage the formation of moderate Islam by forming alliances with domestic organizations, the U.S. has attempted the same with state-to-state alliances abroad. The U.S. also works to promote the development of certain interpretations of Islam for national security, but from behind the scenes. Indonesia and the Philippines provide excellent case studies of how the U.S. used the promotion of moderate Islam as a way to shore up alliances in the War on Terror. In contrast to Britain and France, where civil society resisted secular state intrusion into matters of religion, the U.S. was able through its state allies to encourage the creation of a moderate form of Islam; dealing with any resistance to such a project falls for the most part on the foreign state. For their part, states such as the Philippines and Indonesia accept the necessity of promoting moderate Islam for reasons of national security and also because such a project help both states to increase their geopolitical standing in the region. As I showed in chapter 5, Jordan and Kuwait, too, partnered with the U.S. in order to promote moderate Islam for very much the same reasons. As chapter 5 also showed, unlike in Britain and France, it is the military and defense establishments of the U.S. that have taken the lead in the securitization of religion. A successful securitization is one in which a relevant audience accepts the framing of a threat, a referent, and the policies that flow from them; based on this criterion, Britain and France constitute cases of failure and the U.S., a case of success.

What are the differences between international- and domestic-level securitizations of religion that can account for the different outcomes we see? Securitizations of religions tend to fail at the domestic level of analysis for three reasons. First, as secular states such as Britain and France rush to partner with religious organizations in times when national security is perceived to be under threat, those organizations that cooperate with the state and take on the task of religion-building face a legitimacy crisis in the eyes of civil society. They are perceived as doing the state's bidding and as extensions of the state's security agenda and even its agencies. Alliances between the secular state and religious organizations are risky for both, and tension between the two is inevitable. State-supported representative religious organizations crowd out others and, in the eyes of many, cheapen or politicize—perhaps, securitize—the faith. Second, as the case studies in this book have shown, many religious leaders resent the implication that the loyalty of their organizations is made contingent on accepting and promoting a certain interpretation of their religion. Matters of political obligation are tied up with one's religious faith. For many, this seems to be too high a price to pay for working with the state to protect national security. Finally, particularly regarding the discursive dimensions of the securitization of religion, the very category of moderate Islam itself becomes suspect, tainted because is instrumentalized by both the state and opportunistic organizations seeking access to state power and funds. For these reasons domestic-level securitizations of religion seem particularly prone to failure. In cases in which the secular state can remain behind the scenes, so to speak, and work with foreign allies in promoting moderate Islam abroad, this benefits both states, adds some ideological glue to their alliance, and is in the security interests of both. Any backlash or resistance to the reformation of religion for national security can be absorbed by the foreign state.

In considering the successes and failures of the securitization of religion in comparative perspective, one can also perceive something else: a common and perhaps paradoxical cycle in which engagement with religion tests the limits of secularism. Britain mixed and matched discourses and policies directed toward intelligence gathering and policing with those designed to promote community cohesion through shoring up religious faith. In France, Sarkozy sought to formalize the state's relationship with its Muslim communities for national security purposes and lead a more extensive engagement with religion on the part of the secular state within the larger context of his tinkering with the limits of *laicite*. The United States channels its engagement with religion through the army and the defense establishment but also engages religious ideas and actors in its wider system of alliances with regional allies, raising hackles over the separation of church and state in U.S. foreign policy. Taken as a whole, all three of these cases suggest that the more Western secular states try to engage religious ideas and actors in the public sphere, the more they place their own secular arrangements under pressure.

It is important to acknowledge that this argument may assume too stark a distinction between the secular and the sacred. Many scholars have argued in fact that Euro-American secularism itself has religious foundations and exhibits enduring religious qualities. Indeed, "the line between secular nationalism and religion has always been quite thin," argues Mark Juergensmeyer (1993, 16). Elizabeth Shakman Hurd captures the overall argument nicely when she writes, "the norms and forms" of secularism "emerged out of and remain indebted to both Enlightenment and Christian (and later Judeo-Christian) beliefs and practices" (Hurd 2008, 47 + ff.). Similar arguments can be found in the Muslim tradition. Conservative Islamist discourse often regarded Western secularism as a "foreign and alien," as the particular outgrowth of the European Judeo-Christian tradition (Ismail 2003, 42–3). According to this line of thinking Europe's trajectory does not represent a negation of religion at all, but rather a transformation into a more mundane and immanent form of religion (Shariati 1981). More recently, in a more accomodationist vein, some scholars argue that secularism and religion need each other and can be mutually sustaining (An-Na'im 2008). The meaning and stability of the concept of the secular thus depend very much on one's point of view.

Nonetheless, the securitization of religion can be seen as a collection of instances in which secularism is challenged or nearly suspended for reasons of national security. U.S. military lawyers seem far less concerned than State Department lawyers about whether the constitutional separation of church and state prohibits the U.S. from engaging with religious actors abroad. In France especially, a large part of the backlash against positive *laicite* consisted of Muslim organizations seeking to protect, not resist, France's longstanding tradition of *laicite* out of fear that increased engagement by the state would lead to manipulation of religion. In trying to handle religion in a post–9/11 world, Sarkozy stretched *laicite* too far. The imperatives of national security can indeed push secularism to its limits. The more secular states engage with religious ideas and actors in the public sphere out of a concern for national security, the more this securitization of religion will be perceived as a threat by secularism's resolute defenders, which often include religious organizations. I will return to this point later.

WESTERN STATES AND ISLAM

From the foregoing empirical analysis we can also draw some tentative general conclusions about Western state engagement with the religion of Islam. It is common in the academy to lambast political power for portraying Islam as a monolith. In fact, "Islam is not monolithic" has become something of a required utterance in the academy, it being understood that this insight alone is enough to set apart we academics who know better from the policymakers who do not. However, as I show in this book, when one looks at the evidence, Western secular states do not at all present Islam as a monolithic religion. The reality is not quite this convenient but is in fact precisely the opposite: what is framed as a threat to the security of the Western secular liberal project, is not Islam's monolithic unity but its exceptional diversity and radical openness to different interpretations. Above all, the Western secular state fears believers taking the interpretation of their religion into their own hands. The entire point of the securitization of religion is to channel the development of faith for precisely this reason. The real battleground, as political elites say quite openly, is not in fact violent terrorism but on the terrain of ideas; the battle is a *hermeneutic* one. The paradox of the situation is that the effort is underway to help believers come to see their religion as a matter of interpretation: this is crucial to the task of securitization of religion. As one French security document argued, "only an objective and detailed knowledge of religious traditions and texts can make it possible for young people of all faiths to avoid falling under the sway of extremists distorting the message of their faith, by applying historical, political and social analysis to religions" (La France Face Au Terrorisme 2006, 104). In other words, because the nation is threatened by a religion that can be interpreted in any way by any one given the recent globalization of technology, the state must counteract this by promoting an imminent reading of religion as culturally, politically, and socially relative. So while the state wishes believers to see their religion as a matter of interpretation, interpretation has its limits. Much like the Cold War example of humanistic religion referenced in chapter 1, after 9/11 the West's immanent approach to understanding religion also has an important national security function.

As I mentioned previously, however, it is not that Western security discourse manufactures its referent objects from nothing. It channels and borrows, commandeers and steers preexisting narratives into the territory of security. Religion appears as mercurial, slippery, and viral, like the networked enemy of U.S. military speeches and manuals. Islam can be interpreted in any number of ways and it can also link up with its fellow Judeo-Christian ethical systems or morph into more sinister variants that prey on those with the weakest understanding of their own faith. Islam is political, but its future is at risk. In the post–9/11 global battlefield of the mind and soul, religion is both stable and unstable; a durable feature of the post–9/11 world but evolving and changing unpredictably. Such a new security situation requires a network-centric response, religious factor analyses, total situational awareness, smart power and "forensic theology" (Grey 2004). Religion is represented and dealt with in ways appropriate for an age of network-centric warfare. There are elements of continuity, too, for underpinning Western state engagement with religion and especially Islam is a sunny optimism that such smart power engagement is in the best interests of all. As Bernard Lewis put it in a 2007 speech to the American Enterprise Institute, it is based on the assumption that Muslims "are keenly and painfully aware of their relative backwardness and welcome the opportunity to rectify it" (Lewis 2007). Western secular state engagement with religion requires a transformation of traditional security thinking, but such transformations occur in the context of larger, historically sedimented assumptions about religion and Islam that cannot easily be shaken off. In engaging with religion for national security, Western states thus grapple with their own latent Orientalisms (Said 1979).

Western discourse on Islam—especially U.S. discourse—has a ripple effect. Other nations have begun to internalize and make use of the United States' hastily constructed and ever-shifting post–9/11 categories such as moderate, radical, mainstream, or extremist versions of Islam to reassert their control over the content of what is learned, taught, and said. In Bahrain, the kingdom has recently decided to reassert its control over the state's mosques in order to "ensure that places of worship are run by those who promote the values of tolerance and moderation" (*Kuwait Times* 2010). In China, the Chinese state closely monitors what imams preach. One prominent imam in China recently complained that "we are ordered to preach the concept of peace to believers and to explain to them what harm is done to Muslims by the terrorists who operate in the name of our religion" (Rotar 2010). The problem here is not peace, but that it is increasingly easy for governments to exert control over what is said and taught—the only *content* of religion— under the protection of categories and classifications of Islam promoted by the West itself. Similar developments are taking place in Pakistan, Kenya, Saudi Arabia, Australia, and Ethiopia.

Indeed, religious categories—not just religious organizations—play an important role in state-to-state security arrangements. They may fill a variety of political ends in a world populated by states. They can help solidify alliances. Following 9/11, religion is a potential new deliverable in national security arrangements, opening up new spaces for cooperation and negotiation. This means that the hard core of security—coercive force—can be employed that much more easily. As I alluded to earlier, it can always be argued that there are of course plenty of religious individuals and organizations that consider themselves moderate. Categories such as moderate Islam have an independent function in international politics following 9/11 regardless of how much such categories actually correspond to any underlying sociological reality. That is why discourses on religion and the way they function in international affairs should be as much a part of the study of religion in global politics as the activity of religious organizations or the effect of religious beliefs or norms on individual or collective behaviors.

RELIGION: THE "SMARTEST POWER OF ALL"?

But what does it mean to say that the securitization of religion failed here but succeeded there? This is awkward terminology to use, to be sure, because both terms have obvious normative implications. A serious question arises, however, when we recall that according to the Copenhagen approach, for securitization to succeed—meaning a relevant audience accepts it—may not necessarily be a good thing. Similarly, when securitization fails—a relevant audience resists the way an issue is framed—this may in fact be for the better.

Throughout this book I have attempted to use securitization theory in a nonnormative way. In its classical iteration, securitization theory defines a *successful* securitization as one in which political elites *convince* a relevant audience that a posited threat is indeed of such consequence that exceptional countermeasures are justified. Yet because securitizations often result in confrontational discourses of us versus them, raising an issue above the realm of normal political contestation and into the realm of security is considered dangerous or undesirable from the perspective of the theory (Buzan, Waever, and de Wilde 1998, 4). This book illustrates that analytical differentiation between levels of analysis provides a method to apply securitization theory comparatively and obviates the need to make normative judgments. As such, successes and failures are not conceptualized normatively in this book; rather, these terms represent a state's ability or inability to withstand the inevitable resistance generated by securitizing moves, especially in the religious field.

I will now, however, take up the normative element and show where it might lead. Recall that according to securitization theory, more security is not necessarily a universally good thing. This is because securitizations create antagonisms, divisions between friend and foe, us and them. Securitizations are confrontational. They can breed unnecessary conflict or justify suspensions of the normal restraints of the law. In other words, securitizations separate friends from the enemy and invite the state to override democratic procedures. The normative goal is thus to reclaim the issue from the security realm and return it to the normal run of political contestation where it belongs. In this way, sovereign decisionism will be constrained by open debate, as it should be. Let us follow through some of the normative implications of securitization theory in this case.

One implication is that the United States' success in promoting moderate Islam abroad is not to be celebrated. From this point of view, religion in U.S. foreign policy is a way for the world hegemon to divert attention from its own human-rights violations, botched invasions, militarization of far reaches of the globe, and the rest of the sordid catalogue of empire. Promoting moderate Islam is a way to manipulate others into accepting the global exercise of America's hard power. It is perhaps no coincidence that as U.S. foreign policy becomes increasingly militarized it becomes increasingly concerned with religion, too.

The former head of Chicago Theological Seminary, Susan Thistlewaite, called religion the "smartest power of all" (Thistlewaite 2010). What did she have in mind? That a religion-wielding America will be instantly credible? The problem here is that religion as smart power represents precisely the same paradox that the smart bomb does: its lethality undermines any pretense to a more humane conduct of war. Religion, too, when openly proclaimed by a hypermilitarized global power, is a paper-thin veneer for the exercise of violence. There is the open contradiction: recall Abu Ghraib, Guantanamo Bay, Bagram, CIA black sites; the powerful state trumpets the affinity between Islam and its own cherished values but there is no religious or ethical restraint as the state attempts to achieve security by any means necessary. It seems that the more the state proclaims the virtues of religion for national security the more we can be confident of the death of any "post–Westphalian era of global coexistence" founded on shared religious values.

From the perspective of securitization theory, this implies that perhaps religion does not belong in the context of security. Perhaps it is better that securitizations of religions fail. If the normative objective is to *desecuritize* religion, then from this point of view Britain and France are success stories. It would be better that *laicite* is left alone, because to increase state engagement with religion through positive *laicite* is only to invite manipulation of the latter. Indeed, if one takes the normative component of securitization theory seriously, then there is an argument to be made that it is best to strengthen secularism and reinforce the arrangements that protect religion from the state. It could further be argued that the American variety of secularism, designed to do precisely this, is a good model to follow. The problem arises when efforts to promote the virtues of the U.S. method of protecting religion from state interference are bundled with efforts toward democracy promotion, human rights, or regime change. Here we arrive at a fundamental tension in the securitization of religion whereby Western states, in their attempts to engage and influence religion in the public sphere for reasons of national security, push against the limits of their secular arrangements. At the same time, the state inadvertently unleashes forces in civil society that wish to entrench secularism ever more deeply to guard against state intervention in matters of faith. In such a situation the desirability of the securitization of religion's success or failure is a complex question indeed.

If the Western state's attempts to bring religion in to global affairs sends secularism's defenders running for the ramparts this would constitute a great irony for scholars of religion and international relations. It suggests, first and foremost, that sweeping analyses of religion's potential to spark a wholesale conceptual revolution in the study of international politics seem hyperbolic. Clearly, the international system is no longer an exclusively secular one, if it ever was. On the other hand, it seems equally implausible that the increasing importance of religious ideas and actors in global politics will lead to a moral, post–Westphalian future world order. The truth is in between. As secular political powers attempt to engage and control religion for security they create new cycles of backlash from religious groups that force the state to further engage with religion, challenging its secular foundations. Indeed, the relationship between the sovereign state and religion is a contradiction that, since the Reformation, has never been resolved.

To round out this discussion of the normative questions raised by this study, one must consider the relationship between the analyst and the larger context in which he or she works. From the perspective of securitization theory, this is a crucial matter. As Western states grapple more and more with the matter of religion as a security priority, the more they call upon scholars to help produce *strategically useful knowledge*, blurring the lines between knowledge and power. The American Psychological Association recently passed through a difficult and controversial period because some of its members were using their professional credentials, knowledge, and expertise to advise the U.S. military and security services on the interrogation of detainees at Guantanamo Bay. As of this writing I know of no such controversy at the American Academy of Religion, but it is not too difficult to imagine. It is well established that certain taboos within Islam, particularly among Muslim males, have been deliberately violated by interrogators to emotionally unsettle and disorient detainees. Incorporating religious taboos into enhanced interrogation techniques requires at least some level of nuanced knowledge of religion. An extreme case, to be sure, but the reader would be well served to think of this book as an exploration of a series of variations on this same basic theme. Indeed, it should be borne in mind that the use of religion in interrogation—as well as Bible inscriptions on U.S. weapons, desecrations of the Koran, etc.—is yet another piece of the wider securitization of religion that I try to capture in this book. The incorporation of religious themes and tactics into the techniques of the national security state is one way that states bring religion back in to international politics that should not be overlooked.

Exactly how far then should scholars of religion or scholars of security go in assisting the state in understanding and engaging religious ideas and actors? This type of normative question comes up often from the perspective of securitization theory. Scholarly analysis, including security analysis, is indeed "mostly performed in already heavily politicized contexts" (Huysmans 2002). The case of religion is no different. Raising religion to the status of a policy priority in the name of national security exerts a strong gravitational pull on the academy, blurring the lines between objective and strategic knowledge and creating an environment in which scholars may become unwitting apologists for hard power coercion. After all, soft power is not meant to replace hard power, but to complement and help legitimize it, and smart power is a combination of both. Smart power requires academic knowledge to help fulfill national strategic objectives. Given this, scholars should think carefully when religion is celebrated as "the smartest power of all."

Afterword

Religion presents secular states with a variation on the classic security dilemma: if states accept the premise that religious actors and ideas are matters of national security, then refusing to engage with religion—doing nothing—is not a sensible response. On the other hand, any action taken is likely to heighten *in*security on all sides. When secular, liberal democracies engage with religious actors in the name of national security, they risk becoming involved in interpretive questions regarding religion. This is especially true when states fund the development and dissemination of religious "counter-narratives," because public declamations about what constitutes "correct" or "authentic" meanings of religion necessarily involve differentiating between acceptable and unacceptable religious interpretations. In the cases of Britain and France, counter-narrative initiatives undertaken directly by the state, or by third-party actors funded by it, led to accusations of government social engineering of religion. To be sure, these initiatives had supporters as well as detractors. But this was cold comfort as it only heightened suspicion among Muslim communities that they were being pitted against themselves.

The United States now faces exactly the same dilemma at home. In 2010, U.S. Attorney General Eric Holder told ABC News, "the threat has changed from simply worrying about foreigners coming here, to worrying about people in the United States . . . American citizens, raised here, born here, and who for whatever reason, have decided that they are going to become radicalized and take up arms against the nation in which they were born" (Cloherty and Thomas 2010). Holder's remarks may have been designed partly to prepare the American public for the assassination of U.S. citizen

Anwar Al-Awlaki that occurred soon after, but Holder's warning proved to be accurate. In 2014, four young women from Colorado were intercepted in Germany, allegedly *en route* to join ISIS in Syria. In February 2015, three men from New York were arrested, again for trying to join ISIS. The next month, two men in Illinois, one a former National Guard member, were accused of attempting to provide material support to ISIS and attack a military installation in Illinois. Throughout 2014 and 2015, the U.S. Justice Department publicly revealed 32 cases of Americans attempting to travel abroad to support ISIS and other groups, or to attack the United States or its allies. Two days before I began work on this Afterword, news broke of the ISIS-inspired shooting in San Bernardino, California.

Following 9/11, the U.S. government embarked on an underfunded and disorganized effort to engage with Muslim community leaders. Since then, increasing recruitment of Americans to the ranks of the Islamic State suggests that extremism inspired by religion can be effectively countered by fostering alternative interpretations of Islam. Recent U.S. government efforts to this end are better marketed, better coordinated, and receive far more money and resources than before. In August 2011, the White House developed a counter-extremism strategy entitled "Empowering Local Partners to Prevent Violent Extremism in the United States," which was the first national strategy to prevent violent extremism domestically (White House 2011a). This was followed in December of the same year by a "Strategic Implementation Plan for Empowering Local Partners to Prevent Violent Extremism in the United States," which outlines the specific initiatives U.S. agencies will take to achieve the program's goals (White House 2011b). The effort involves the Department of Homeland Security, the Department of Justice, the FBI, and the National Counterterrorism Center, and has three major goals: to support communities likely to be targeted by extremists, build law enforcement expertise to prevent violent extremism, and counter violent extremist propaganda while promoting U.S. ideals. It includes specific initiatives to raise awareness of "violent extremism," facilitate intervention into person(s) seemingly on the path to radicalization, and develop counter-narratives. Community outreach is central. In 2014–15, the Department of Justice, the FBI, and the Department of Homeland Security started pilot outreach programs in Boston, Los Angeles, and the Twin Cities. Indeed, today's U.S. government programs to engage Muslim communities in the U.S. are far better funded and more coherent than the haphazard, panicked efforts put in place after 9/11. But are they more effective?

These current U.S. government-led initiatives resemble British and

French ones, and given the patterns revealed in this book, it is reasonable to expect they will encounter the same problems. As in Britain and France, a key part of the U.S. strategy is to counter "violent extremist ideology" with credible counter-narratives, which can defeat ideologies stemming from isolation or disenchantment, both of which can feed the notion that the United States is at war with Islam. Again, just as in the cases of the U.K. and France, the U.S. has emphasized that such counter-radicalization programs do not constitute government intervention into religion. The 2011 "Empowering Local Partners to Prevent Violent Extremism" report states that "strong religious beliefs should never be confused with violent extremism" (White House 2011a, 8). Countering Violent Extremism guidance issued by the Department of Homeland Security states that "training should focus on behavior, not appearance or membership in particular ethnic or religious communities" (quoted in Bjelopera 2014). Qualifications aside, however, the U.S. counter-radicalization program is now subject to precisely the same criticisms that beset British and French strategies.

When the U.S. government's Countering Violent Extremism Strategy was released in 2011, the Council on American-Islamic Relations responded: "in all three pilot cities, local community leaders who support efforts to secure our nation . . . distanced themselves from the project as they formed a deeper understanding of its problematic realities" (CAIR 2015). In 2015, Yusufi Vali, Executive Director of the Islamic Society of Boston, claimed that he could not support the U.S. government outreach efforts in Boston because the programs "are founded on the premise that your faith determines your propensity towards violence" (Bender 2015). Meanwhile, in the Twin Cities, 50 Muslim organizations banded together to claim that the counter-radicalization program has "focused on people's natural religious expression, labeling them as 'extremist' or 'radical' . . . we therefore believe that it is not the place of government to determine what ideologies or religious opinions are problematic, or to fund or encourage groups that believe they can, to make that determination" (cited at CAIR 2015). At the third pilot site in Los Angeles, reports surfaced of how FBI surveillance began to influence religious practice as more Muslims began to avoid mosques and pray at home. Hussam Ayloush, Executive Director of CAIR, told the *Los Angeles Times* that the new tendency for Muslims to pray at home instead of at the mosque represents "infringement of the free practice of our religion" (Watanabe and Esquivel 2009). Some mosques asked their imams to refrain from any discussion of U.S. foreign policy. The United States Council of Muslim Organizations protested that "religious leaders should feel safe to provide guidance on topics from Islamic sources, to help construct a positive understanding of Islam in at-risk persons. This includes the need to discuss domestic abuse of civil liberties and foreign policy issues" (USCMO 2015). As CAIR expresses it, if the U.S. government funds community groups to conduct Countering Violent Extremism programs, this "places the government in the position of 'white listing' ideologies of which it approves and, by extension, 'black listing' others. The Establishment Clause prohibits any governmental endorsement of a particular religious ideology, let alone funding to promote it" (CAIR 2015). It is worth pointing out that neither CAIR nor the USCMO are in principle opposed to U.S. government-led efforts to reach out to their communities, and both publicly underscore that they are willing partners in efforts to fight extremism. It is, as the other cases in this book have amply demonstrated, a matter of government intervention in religion.

CONCLUSION

Increasing ISIS recruitment of Americans has caused the U.S. to develop a wide ranging, "whole of government" response to violent extremism far beyond the scope of anything tried before. So far, U.S. officials seem to be aware of some of the pitfalls. In his February 2016 speech to the Islamic Society of Baltimore, for example, Barack Obama said "we can't securitize our entire relationship with Muslim Americans. We can't deal with you solely through the prism of law enforcement" (White House 2016). On the other hand, *Securing the Sacred* describes clearly the post-9/11 security dilemma that Western liberal democracies face when dealing with religion. It is mostly a book about failure. Even the 'success' case—the U.S. securitization of religion abroad—was shown to rest on a dubious combination of consent and coercion. Given the clear pattern across cases of good intentions yielding bad results, what can be done?

Secular, democratic governments can and should get out of the business of funding or otherwise encouraging hand-picked religious representatives to disseminate a counter-narrative about Islam, or any other religion. As this book has shown, this is a risky venture because it undermines the legitimacy of both the state and the speaker. Moreover, these sorts of attempts occur in a context of general unease regarding Western—especially American—foreign policy. State-funded religious interlocutors are perceived in that context. A better solution may be the more straightforward one: when it comes to religion, governments should stick to the level of the symbolic. In other words, stop constructing counter-narratives about Islam, and focus more on disseminating the basic message of inclusion, tolerance, and mutual respect. There is no need to tie these national values to a religious form. To do so is effectively to link political obligation to religious interpretation, which is a source of many problems, as I have shown. Britain learned this lesson the hard way. In 2010, after an exhaustive review of the PREVENT programs shortcomings, Britain's House of Commons admitted the country's counter-radicalization programs focused far too much on theological and religious issues to the neglect of political or socioeconomic ones. The United States should heed the experience of Britain. Note that this does not preclude dialogue between the secular state and religious communities, or training diplomats or law enforcement to understand religion and culture better. All this should be encouraged. But secular, liberal democracies should stick to doing the things they should, in theory, do best: exercise self-restraint in matters of faith and religion, and focus instead on making a very public case for toleration, civility, and cosmopolitanism.

WORKS CITED

Bjelopera, Lerome P. 2014. "Countering Violent Extremism in the United States." Congressional Research Service Report R42553, February 19.
Bender, Bryan. 2015. "Islamic Leader Says U.S. Officials Unfairly Target Muslims." *Boston Globe*, February 18. http://www.bostonglobe.com/news/nation/2015/02/18/islamic-leader-boston-says-justice-department-effort-iden tify-homegrown-terrorists-unfairly-targeting-muslim-community/uqzG0M3c zJeuVH8HhSDtRN/story.html
Cloherty, Jack, and Pierre Thomas. 2010. "Attorney General Issues Blunt Warning on Terror Attacks." *ABC News*, December 21. http://abcnews.go.com/Politics/attorney-general-eric-holders-blunt-warning-terror-attacks/story?id=12444727
CAIR (Council on American-Islamic Relations). 2015. "Brief on Countering Violent Extremism." http://www.cair.com/government-affairs/13063-brief-on-countering-violent-extremism-cve.html
USCMO (U.S. Council of Muslim Organizations). 2015. "Muslim Council Adopts Points on Countering Violent Extremism." http://www.shuracouncil.org/Shura/USCMO_On_CVE_Statement.pdf
Watanabe, Teresa, and Paloma Esquivel. 2009. "L.A. Area Muslims Say FBI Surveillance Has a Chilling Effect on Religious Practices." *Los Angeles Times*, March 1.
White House. 2011a. "Empowering Local Partners to Prevent Violent Extremism in the United States." https://www.whitehouse.gov/sites/default/files/empower ing_local_partners.pdf

White House. 2011b. "Strategic Implementation Plan for Empowering Local Partners to Prevent Violent Extremism in the United States." https://www.white house.gov/sites/default/files/sip-final.pdf

White House. 2016. "Remarks by the President at Islamic Society of Baltimore." Available at www.whitehouse.gov

Notes

INTRODUCTION

1. *Laicism* is a form of secularity that refers mainly to the deliberate (and often coerced) exclusion of religious expression and argumentation from the public political domain. It envisions and enforces religion as a private matter. While *laicism* understands itself to represent the culmination of Enlightenment attempts to definitively surpass the retrograde impulses of religion, Judeo-Christian secularism maintains that "Christianity informs and sustains the moral foundations of the modern secular order" (Hurd 2008, 27). For a fuller discussion of varieties of secularism, see Hurd 2008, especially 29–37.

2. Elizabeth Shakman Hurd uses the phrase "securitization of religion" in a post on *The Immanent Frame,* but my usage of the term is substantially wider than hers. Compare Elizabeth Shakman Hurd, "The Global Securitization of Religion," March 23, 2010, The Immanent Frame website, http://blogs.ssrc.org/tif/2010/03/23/global-securitization/.

3. "7/7" refers to the suicide bombings of July 7, 2005, in London's Underground, which killed over 50 civilians and the attackers. The attacks were significant not only for the loss of life but because they represented the first large-scale suicide attack on British soil by "home-grown" British Muslim extremists. 7/7 provided much of the impetus for the British government's counterterrorism policies I review in this book.

CHAPTER 3

1. A traveling program for young people called "Radical Middle Way" also received state funds. According to its website, the Radical Middle Way program promotes a "mainstream, moderate understanding of Islam that young people can relate to . . . our work fosters more open, engaged and cohesive communities."

References

Abdul Bari, Muhammad. 2008. "The Role of Muslims in Constructing a Better Britain." 24 April.

Abu-Rabi, Ibrahim M. 1996. *Intellectual Origins of Islamic Resurgence in the Modern Arab World.* New York: State University of New York Press.

Amiraux, Valerie. 2003. "CFCM: A French Touch?" *ISIM Newsletter* 12 (June): 24–25.

Amselem, W. Lewis. 2006. "Your Visit to Indonesia: Launching a Renewed Bilateral Partnership." U.S. Embassy, Jakarta, 3 January. http://www.wikileaks.org/cable/2006/01/06JAKARTA59.html. Accessed May 19, 2012.

An-Na'im, Abdullahi Ahmed. 2008. *Islam and the Secular State: Negotiating the Future of Shari'a.* Cambridge MA: Harvard University Press.

Appleby, R. Scott. 2000. *The Ambivalence of the Sacred: Religion, Violence, and Reconciliation.* Lanham, MD: Rowman and Littlefield.

Arts and Humanities Research Council. 2008. "Police-Muslim Engagement and Partnerships for the Purposes of Counter-Terrorism: An Examination." UK: University of Birmingham, 18 November.

Asad, Talal. 1993. *Genealogies of Religion: Discipline and Reasons of Power in Christianity and Islam.* Baltimore: Johns Hopkins University Press.

Badinter, Elisabeth, Regis Debray, Alain Finkielkraut, Elisabeth de Fontenay, and Catherine Kintzler. 1989. "Profs, ne Capitulons Pas!" http://www.mediapart.fr/files/Badinter.pdf. Accessed May 20, 2012.

Baran, Zeyno, ed. 2004. "Understanding Sufism and its Potential Role in U.S. Policy." Nixon Center Conference Report. Washington, DC: Nixon Center.

Bastiere, Jean-Marc. 2008. "Nicolas Sarkozy, Laiquement Incorrect." *Le Figaro,* 27 June.

BBC News. 2009. "UK to Shift Anti-Terror Strategy." 16 February. http://news.bbc.co.uk/2/hi/7889631.stm. Accessed May 19, 2012.

Bedsole, Timothy K. 2006. "Religion: The Missing Dimension in Mission Planning." *Special Warfare* 19, no. 6 (November–December): 8–15.

Benard, Cheryl. 2003. "Civil Democratic Islam: Partners, Resources, and Strategies." Santa Monica, CA: RAND Corporation.

Berger, Peter, ed. 1999. *The Desecularization of the World: Resurgent Religion and World Politics.* Grand Rapids, MI: William B. Eerdmans/Ethics and Public Policy Center.

Berkley Center for Religion, Peace & World Affairs. 2010. "Report of the Georgetown Symposium on Religious Freedom and National Security Policy." 28 October.

Berkley Center for Religion, Peace & World Affairs. 2010–2011. "Annual Report."

Blair, Tony. 2006. "Speech on the Middle East to the Los Angeles World Affairs Council." http://www.number10.gov.uk/Page9948. Accessed April 15, 2010.

Blair, Tony. 2007. "Speech at the International Conference on Islam and Muslims." http://www.number10.gov.uk/Page11826. Accessed April 15, 2010.

Blair, Tony. 2009. "Speech to the Chicago Council on Global Affairs." http://www.tonyblairoffice.org/speeches/entry/tony-blair-speech-to-chicago-council-on-global-affairs/. Accessed April 15, 2010.

Blaschke, Karlheinz, 1986. "The Reformation and the Rise of the Territorial State." In *Luther and the Modern State in Germany,* edited by James D. Tracy, 61–75. Kirksville, MO: Sixteenth Century Journal Publisher.

Blears, Hazel. 2007. "Preventing Extremism: Strengthening Communities." http://www.communities.gov.uk/speeches/corporate/preventingextremism. Accessed April 15, 2010.

Blears, Hazel. 2008a. "Preventing Violent Extremism: Next Steps for Communities." http://www.communities.gov.uk/news/corporate/898004. Accessed April 15, 2010.

Blears, Hazel. 2008b. "Local Government Association Conference on Preventing Violent Extremism." http://www.communities.gov.uk/speeches/corporate/preventing. Accessed April 15, 2010.

Blears, Hazel. 2009. "Many Voices: Understanding the Debate About Preventing Violent Extremism." http://www.communities.gov.uk/speeches/corporate/manyvoices. Accessed April 15, 2010.

Bosco, Robert M. 2009. "Persistent Orientalisms: The Concept of Religion in International Relations." *Journal of International Relations and Development* 12 (1): 90–111.

Bosco, Robert M., and Lori Hartmann-Mahmud. 2011. "The Securitization of Park51." *Peace Review: Journal of Social Justice* 23, no. 4 (October–December): 530–36.

Bowen, John R. 2004. "Does French Islam Have Borders? Dilemmas of Domestication in a Global Religious Field." *American Anthropologist* 106 (1): 43–55.

Briggs, Rachel, Catherine Fieschi, and Hannah Lownsbrough. 2006. "Bringing it Home: Community-Based Approaches to Counter-Terrorism." London: Demos.

Bryant, Lisa. 2008. "France Starts Muslim Imam Training." *Voice of America,* 9 March.

Bush, George W. 2001a. "Address to the Nation on the September 11 Attacks." 11 September. In *Selected Speeches of President George W. Bush*. http://georgewbush-whitehouse.archives.gov/infocus/bushrecord/. Accessed May 19, 2012.

Bush, George W. 2001b. "National Day of Prayer and Remembrance Service." 14 September. In *Selected Speeches of President George W. Bush*. http://georgewbush-whitehouse.archives.gov/infocus/bushrecord/. Accessed May 19, 2012.

Bush, George W. 2001c. "Address to the Joint Session of the 107th Congress." 20 September. In *Selected Speeches of President George W. Bush*. http://georgewbush-whitehouse.archives.gov/infocus/bushrecord/. Accessed May 19, 2012.

Bush, George W. 2001d. "Address at the Islamic Center of Washington." 17 September. www.americanrhetoric.com. Accessed May 19, 2012.

Bush, George W. 2001e. "Department of Defense Service of Remembrance at the Pentagon." 11 October. In *Selected Speeches of President George W. Bush*. http://georgewbush-whitehouse.archives.gov/infocus/bushrecord/. Accessed May 19, 2012.

Bush, George W. 2001f. "Address to the United Nations General Assembly." 10 November. In *Selected Speeches of President George W. Bush*. http://georgewbush-whitehouse.archives.gov/infocus/bushrecord/. Accessed May 19, 2012.

Bush, George W. 2003. "Remarks of the Freedom Agenda." 6 November. In *Selected Speeches of President George W. Bush*. http://georgewbush-whitehouse.archives.gov/infocus/bushrecord/. Accessed 19 May 2012.

Bush, George W. 2005a. "Speech at the National Endowment for Democracy." 6 October. http://www.presidentialrhetoric.com/speeches/10.06.05.print.html. Accessed May 19, 2012.

Bush, George W. 2005b. "The Second Inaugural Address." 20 January. In *Selected Speeches of President George W. Bush*. http://georgewbush-whitehouse.archives.gov/infocus/bushrecord/. Accessed May 19, 2012.

Bush, George W. 2006a. "The Ideological Struggle of the 21st Century." 31 August. In *Selected Speeches of President George W. Bush*. Available at: http://georgewbush-whitehouse.archives.gov/infocus/bushrecord/. Accessed May 19, 2012.

Bush, George W. 2006b. "Remarks on the Global War on Terror: The Enemy in Their Own Words." 5 September. In *Selected Speeches of President George W. Bush*. http://georgewbush-whitehouse.archives.gov/infocus/bushrecord/. Accessed May 19, 2012.

Bush, George W. 2007. "Address to the Nation on Iraq." 10 January. In *Selected Speeches of President George W. Bush*. http://georgewbush whitehouse.archives.gov/infocus/bushrecord/. Accessed May 19, 2012.

Buzan, Barry, Ole Waever and Jaap de Wilde. 1998. "Security: A New Framework." Boulder: Lynne Rienner.

Caeiro, Alejandro. 2005. "Religious Authorities or Political Actors? The Muslim Leaders of the French Representative Body of Islam." In *European Muslims and the Secular State*, edited Jocelyn Cesari and Sean McLaughlin, 71–84. Aldershot UK: Ashgate.

Campbell, David. 1992. *Writing Security: United States Foreign Policy and the Politics of Identity.* Minneapolis: University of Minnesota Press.

Casanova, Jose. 1994. *Public Religions in the Modern World.* Chicago: University of Chicago Press.

Casciani, Dominic. 2008. "Government Funds Muslim Thinkers." *BBC News,* 18 July.

Cavanaugh, William T. 1995. "A Fire Strong Enough to Consume the House: The Wars of Religion and the Rise of the State." *Modern Theology* 11 (4): 397–420.

Center for Strategic and International Studies. 2007a. "A Smarter, More Secure America." Washington, DC: Center for Strategic and International Studies.

Center for Strategic and International Studies. 2011. "What the COIN Manual Says about Religion." http://csis.org/blog/what-coin-manual-says-about-religion. Accessed May 20, 2012.

Cesari, Jocelyne. 2004. *When Islam and Democracy Meet: Muslims in Europe and in the United States.* New York: Palgrave.

Cesari, Jocelyne. 2009. "The Securitisation of Islam in Europe." *Challenge Research Paper No. 14,* April, 1–14.

Charlton, Emma. 2005. "Sarkozy Calls for Change to 1905 Secularity Law." *Middle East Online,* 31 October.

Choudhury Tufyal, and Helen Fenwick. 2011. "The Impact of Counter-Terrorism Measures on Muslim Communities." Manchester: Equality and Human Rights Commission.

Chicago Council on Global Affairs. 2010. "Engaging Religious Communities Abroad: A New Imperative for U.S. Foreign Policy." Chicago: Chicago Council on Global Affairs.

Connexion France. 2011. "Religions Unite Against UMP Debate." http://www.con nexionfrance.com/France-religion-debate-jews-christians-muslims-buddhists-UMP-view-article.html. Accessed May 20, 2012.

Courter, Ian, Ron Fiegle, and Buford Shofner. 2007. "Religious Factors Analysis: A New Emphasis and a New Approach." *Special Warfare* 20, no. 10 (January–February): 25–30.

Croft, Stuart. 2012. *Securitizing Islam: Identity and the Search for Security.* Cambridge: Cambridge University Press.

Curtis, Michael. 2009. *Orientalism and Islam: European Thinkers on Oriental Despotism in the Middle East and India.* Cambridge: Cambridge University Press.

Davie, Grace. 1994. *Religion in Britain Since 1945: Believing Without Belonging.* Oxford: Blackwell.

Defense et Securite Nationale. 2008. New York: Odile Jacob, La Documentation Francaise. Available in English at http://www.ambafranceca.org/IMG/pdf/ Livre_blanc_Press_kit_english_version.pdf. Accessed May 20, 2012.

Department of Children, Schools, and Families. 2007. "Islamic Studies to become a 'Strategic Subject' in Higher Education." http://dcsf.gov.uk./pns/DisplayPN. cgi?pn_id=2007_0099.

De Villepin, Dominique. 2003. "Speech to the Eleventh Ambassadors Conference." http://www.ambafrance-uk.org/Eleventh-Ambassadors-Conference,4765.html.

Dodd, Vikram. 2009. "Anti-Terror Code Would Alienate Most Muslims." *Guardian,* 17 February.

Eckert, William. 2006. "Defeating the Idea: Unconventional Warfare in the Southern Philippines." *Special Warfare* 19, no. 6 (November-December): 16–22.

Eickelman, Dale. 1997. "Trans-state Islam and Security." In *Transnational Religion and Fading States*, edited by Susan Hoeber Rudolph and James Piscatori. Boulder: Westview Press.

Entous, Adam, and Phil Stewart. 2010. "Exclusive: The Warrior-Scholar Versus the Taliban." *Reuters*. 25 June 2010. http://www.reuters.com/article/2010/06/25/us-petraeus-idUSTRE65O0R820100625. Accessed September 19, 2010.

Erlanger, Steven, and Maia de la Baume. 2011. "French Panel Debates Secularism and Islam." *New York Times,* 6 April.

Esposito, John L., ed. 1987. *Islam in Asia.* New York: Oxford University Press.

Esposito, John L. 1992. *The Islamic Threat: Myth or Reality?* New York: Oxford University Press.

Eteraz, Ali. 2009. "State-Sponsored Sufism." *Foreign Policy,* 10 June.

Farr, Thomas F. 2008. *World of Faith and Freedom: Why International Religious Liberty is Vital to American National Security.* New York: Oxford University Press.

Farr, Thomas F. 2011. Interview with the author, 2 August.

Fernando, Mayanthi. 2005. "The Republic's 'Second Religion': Recognizing Islam in France." *Middle East Report* 235, Summer.

Fierke, Karen M. 2007. *Critical Approaches to International Security.* Cambridge: Polity Press.

Ford, Peter. 2004. "France Tries to Soften Local Style of Islam." *Christian Science Monitor,* 6 May.

Ford, Richard. 2008. "Imams to Counter 'Mistaken' Muslim Beliefs." *Times Online,* 19 July.

Foucault, Michel. [1970] 1994. *The Order of Things: An Archeology of the Human Sciences.* New York: Vintage.

Foucault, Michel. 1991. *The Foucault Effect: Studies in Governmentality.* Edited by Graham Burchell, Colin Gordon, and Peter Miller. Chicago: University of Chicago Press.

Fox, Jonathan, and Schmuel Sandler. 2006. *Bringing Religion into International Relations.* New York: Palgrave.

France 24. 2011. "French Religious Leaders Warn Against Planned Islam Debate." 30 March.

French Council of Muslim Faith. 2011. "Concerns of the CFCM about the New Debate on Secularism." *Online Communique,* 4 March.

Geertz, Clifford. 1968. *Islam Observed.* Chicago: University of Chicago Press.

Guenois, Jean-Marie. 2009. "Joseph Maila, le 'M. Religion' du Quai d'Orsay." *Le Figaro,* 13 October.

Globalist. 2010. "Interview with Joseph Maila, Head of the Ministry of Foreign and European Affairs' Religious Division." http://www.delegfrance-conseil-europe.org/spip.php?article417.

Gnietwotta, Tyler, and Yohanna Ririhena. 2011. "9/11 Pushes Islam, Indonesia to Prominence." *Jakarta Post,* 9 September.

Grey, Stephen. 2004. "Follow the Mullahs." *Atlantic.* November. http://www.the atlantic.com/doc/print/200411/grey. Accessed April 10, 2009.

Haddad, Yvonne Yazbeck, and Michael J. Balz. 2008. "Taming the Imams: European Governments and Islamic Preachers Since 9/11." *Islam and Christian-Muslim Relations* 19, no. 2 (April): 215–35.

Haddad, Yvonne and Tyler Golson. 2007. "Overhauling Islam: Representation, Construction, and Cooption of 'Moderate Islam' in Western Europe." *Journal of Church and State* 49 (3): 487–516.

Hansen, Lene. 2006. *Security as Practice: Discourse Analysis and the Bosnian War.* London and New York: Routledge.

Hatzopoulos, Pavlos, and Fabio Petito. 2003. *Religion in International Affairs: The Return from Exile.* New York: Palgrave.

Hayden, Jessica Powley. 2006. "Mullahs on a Bus: The Establishment Clause and U.S. Foreign Aid." *Georgetown Law Journal* 95 (1): 171–206.

HC 65. House of Commons Communities and Local Government Committee. 2010. "Preventing Violent Extremism: Sixth Report of Session 2009–2010." London: The Stationary Office Limited.

Heneghan, Thomas. 2009a. "French Foreign Ministry Bureau Studies Faith Worldwide." *Faithworld: Religion, Faith, and Ethics,* 29 December. http://blogs.reuters.com/faithworld/2009/12/29/french-foreign-ministry-bureau-studies-faith-issues-worldwide/. Accessed May 20, 2012.

Heneghan, Thomas. 2009b. "Europe Talks with Faiths it Once Thought Would Fade." *Reuters,* 29 December. http://www.timesofmalta.com/articles/view/20091229/world/europe-talks-with-faiths-it-once-thought-would-fade.287714. Accessed May 20, 2012.

Heneghan, Thomas. 2011. "French Religious Leaders Warn against Islam Debate." *Reuters,* 30 March. http://in.reuters.com/article/2011/03/30/idINIndia-55990920110330. Accessed May 20, 2012.

Henley, Jon. 2004. "France to Train Imams in 'French Islam.'" *Guardian,* 23 April.

Higgins, Andrew. 2009. "As Indonesia Debates Islam's Role, U.S. Stays Out." *Washington Post,* 28 October.

Hizb ut Tahrir. 2004. "A Letter to the Muslim Community." http://english.hizbut tahrir.org/5-146-20-a-letter-to-the-muslim-community.aspx. Accessed July 11, 2009.

Hourani, Albert. 1983. *Arabic Thought in the Liberal Age 1798–1939.* Cambridge: Cambridge University Press.

Hume, Cameron. 2007. "Political Islam: Mainstream Muslims Condemn 'Caliphate' Idea." U.S. Embassy, Jakarta, 5 November. http://wikileaks.org/cable/2007/11/07JAKARTA3070.html. Accessed February 7, 2002.

Hume, Cameron. 2008a. "Indonesian Counterterrorism and Deradicalization Initiatives." U.S. Embassy, Jakarta, 6 February. http://wikileaks.org/cable/2008/02/08JAKARTA247.html. Accessed February 7, 2002.

Hume, Cameron. 2008b. "Winning the 'War of Ideas' in Indonesia." U.S. Embassy, Jakarta, 5 November. http://www.wikileaks.org/cable/2008/11/08JAKARTA2048.html. Accessed February 7, 2002.

Hume, Cameron. 2008c. "Encouraging Credible Voices to Counter Violent Extremism in Indonesia." U.S. Embassy, Jakarta, 11 December. http://wikileaks.org/cable/2008/12/08JAKARTA2235.html. Accessed February 7, 2002.

Hunter, Shireen T., ed. 2009. *Reformist Voices in Islam*. Armonk, NY: M. E. Sharpe.

Huntington, Samuel P. 1993. "The Clash of Civilizations?" *Foreign Affairs,* Summer.

Hurd, Elizabeth Shakman. 2008. *The Politics of Secularism in International Relations*. Princeton: Princeton University Press.

Huysmans, Jeff. 2002. "Defining Social Constructivism in Security Studies: The Normative Dilemma of Writing Security" *Alternatives* (27): 41–62.

Inboden, William, III. 2010. *Religion and American Foreign Policy, 1945–1960: The Soul of Containment*. Cambridge: Cambridge University Press.

Inboden, William, III. 2011. Interview with the author, 15 November.

International Religious Freedom Act. 1998. 105th Congress of the United States. http://www.gpo.gov/fdsys/pkg/PLAW-105publ292/pdf/PLAW-105publ292.pdf. Accessed May 20, 2012.

Islamonline.net. "U.S. Teaches Afghan Detainees 'Moderate' Islam." 14 June. http://islamonline.com/news/articles/2/US_Teaches_Afghan_Detainees_Moderate_Islam.html. Accessed May 20, 2012.

Islam Today. 2011. "Cope Seeks to Reassure Muslims Before France's National Islam Debate." 22 March.

Ismail, Salwa. 2003. *Rethinking Islamist Politics*. London and New York: I. B. Tauris.

Jenkins, Philip. 2004. "The Politics of Persecuted Religious Minorities." In *Religion and Security: The New Nexus in International Relations,* edited by Robert A. Seiple and Dennis R. Hoover, 25–36. New York: Rowman and Littlefield.

Johnston, Dennis, and Cynthia Sampson, eds. 1994. *Religion: The Missing Dimension of Statecraft*. Oxford: Oxford University Press.

Jones, Paul. 2006. "Philippines: Counterterrorism Assistance (Part 2.)" U.S. Embassy, Manila, 13 January. http://wikileaks.org/cable/2006/01/06MANILA190.html. Accessed January 19, 2012.

Juergensmeyer, Mark. 1993. *The New Cold War? Religious Nationalism Confronts the Secular State*. Berkeley and Los Angeles: University of California Press.

Kaplan, David E. 2005. "Hearts, Minds, and Dollars." *U.S. News and World Report*. April 17. http://www.usnews.com/usnews/news/articles/050425/25roots.htm.

Katzenstein, Peter J. 1996. *The Culture of National Security*. New York: Columbia University Press.

Katzenstein, Peter J. 2006. "Multiple Modernities as Limits to Secular Europeanization?" In *Religion in an Expanding Europe,* edited by Timothy A. Byrnes and Peter J. Katzenstein. Cambridge: Cambridge University Press.

Kaya, Ayhan. 2012. *Islam, Migration, and Securitization*. London: Palgrave.

Kenney, Kristie A. 2006. "Incentives for Peace and Counter-Terrorism Gains in Mindanao." U.S. Embassy, Manila, 6 December. http://www.wikileaks.org/cable/2006/12/06MANILA4915.html. Accessed January 24, 2012.

Kenney, Kristie A. 2008. "Philippine 'Credible Voices' Against Violent Extremism." U.S. Embassy, Manila, 9 December. http://www.wikileaks.org/cable/2008/12/08MANILA2674.html. Accessed January 24, 2012.

Kepel, Gilles. 2004. *The War for Muslim Minds.* Cambridge, MA: Belknap Press.

Kerbaj, Richard. 2009. "Government Moves to Isolate Muslim Council of Britain with Cash for Mosques." *Times Online,* 30 March.

Klausen, Jytte. 2005. *The Islamic Challenge: Politics and Religion in Western Europe.* Oxford and New York: Oxford University Press.

Kuru, Ahmet. 2009. *Secularism and State Policies Toward Religion.* Cambridge: Cambridge University Press.

Kuwait Times. 2010. "Bahrain Reasserts State Control over Mosques." 7 September. http://www.kuwaittimes.net/read_newsphp?newsid=OTgyMzc4MzIo. Accessed September 8, 2010.

La France Face Au Terrorisme. 2006. "La Documentation Francaise." http://www.diplomatie.gouv.fr/fr/IMG/pdf/LIVRE_BLANC_terrorisme.pdf. Accessed May 20, 2012.

Lapidus, Ira M. 2002. *A History of Islamic Societies.* Cambridge: Cambridge University Press.

Laustsen, Carsten Bagge, and Ole Waever. 2003. "In Defense of Religion: Sacred Referent Objects for Securitization." In *Religion in International Relations: The Return from Exile,* edited by Fabio Petito and Pavlos Hatzopoulos, 147–80. New York: Palgrave.

LeBaron, Richard. 2005. "Combating Extremism in Kuwait." U.S. Embassy, Kuwait, 27 September. http://wikileaks.org/cable/2005/09/05KUWAIT4209. html. Accessed January 19, 2012.

LeBaron, Richard. 2006a. "Security Bureau Chief Says Kuwait to be Example of Islamic Moderation; Praises CT Cooperation with Neighbors." U.S. Embassy, Kuwait, 8 February. http://www.wikileaks.org/cable/2006/02/06KUWAIT464. html. Accessed January 19, 2012.

LeBaron, Richard. 2006b. "New Kuwaiti Ministers Pledge to Fight Terror, Promote Moderation." U.S. Embassy, Kuwait, 12 February. http://www.wikileaks.org/cable/2006/02/06KUWAIT490.html. Accessed January 19, 2012.

Leach, Howard H. 2005. "Villepin's Police Advisor Discusses French Internal Security." U.S. Embassy, Paris, 17 March. http://www.wikileaks.org/cable/2005/03/05PARIS1807.html. Accessed October 6, 2011.

Lewis, Bernard. 2007. "The 2007 Irving Kristol Lecture." The American Enterprise Institute, 7 March.

Lilla, Mark. 2007. *The Stillborn God.* New York: Alfred A. Knopf.

Lincoln, Bruce. 1989. *Discourse and Construction of Society.* New York and Oxford: Oxford University Press.

Lincoln, Bruce. 2006. "Bush's God Talk." In *Political Theologies: Public Religions in a Post-Secular World,* edited by Hent de Vries and Lawrence E. Sullivan, 269–77. New York: Fordham University Press.

Lum, Thomas. 2012. "The Republic of the Philippines and U.S. Interests." *Congressional Research Service.* 5 April.

Lynch, Colum. 2009. "In Fighting Radical Islam, Tricky Course for U.S. Aid." *Washington Post,* 30 July.

Maila, Joseph. 2009. "Le pole Religions." *Mondes: Les Cahiers du Quai D'Orsay* 1:104–7.

Marquand, Robert. 2008. "With Pope's Visit, Sarkozy Challenges French Secularism." *Christian Science Monitor,* 15 September.

Marquand, Robert. 2009a. "France President Sarkozy Drops National Identity Debate." *Christian Science Monitor,* 9 February.

Marquand, Robert. 2009b. "Secular France Gives Religion a Seat at the Political Table." *Christian Science Monitor,* 9 September.

Masuzawa, Tomoko. 2005. *The Invention of World Religions.* Chicago: University of Chicago Press.

Mazzetti, Mark. 2010. "U.S. is said to Expand Secret Actions in Mideast." *New York Times.* 24 May.

McCutcheon, Russell T. 2004a. "Just Follow the Money: The Cold War, the Humanistic Study of Religion, and the Fallacy of Insufficient Cynicism." *Culture and Religion* 5 (1): 41–69.

McCutcheon, Russell T. 2004b. "Religion and the Problem of the Governable Self: Or How to Live in a Less than Perfect Nation." *Method and Theory in the Study of Religion* 16:164–81.

McLaughlin, Sean. 2006. "The State, New Muslim Leaderships and Islam as a Resource for Public Engagement in Britain." In *European Muslims and the Secular State,* edited by Jocelyn Cesari and Sean McLaughlin, 55–69. Aldershot, UK: Ashgate.

McNicoll, Tracy. 2008. "The President's Passion Play." *Newsweek,* 9 February.

Milliken, Jennifer. 1999. "The Study of Discourse in International Relations: A Critique of Research and Methods." *European Journal of International Relations* 5 (2): 225–54.

Molnar, Attila K. 2002. "The Construction of the Notion of Religion in Early Modern Europe." *Method and Theory in the Study of Religion* 14:47–60.

Montlake, Simon. 2007. "U.S. Tries Rehab for Religious Extremists." *Christian Science Monitor,* 9 October.

Muslim Council of Britain. 2002. "Response to the Office of National Statistics: Religion: Scoping Report." www.mcb.org. Accessed March 17, 2009.

Muslim Council of Britain, 2008. "Government Approved Theologians Board Will Be Viewed with Scepticism and Mistrust." 18 July.

Muslim Council of Britain. 2011. "Stigmatising Muslim Civil Society Won't Avert Terrorism: Prevent Strategy Still Flawed." http://www.mcb.org.uk/media/presstext.php?ann_id=449. Accessed May 19, 2012.

Muslim Council of Britain. 2013. Muslim Council of Britain Research and Documentation Committee. www.mcb.org.uk/library/studies.php. Accessed January 3, 2013.

Mussomeli, Joseph. 2005. "Fighting the GWOT in the Philippines." U.S. Embassy, Manila, 7 April. http://www.wikileaks.org/cable/2005/04/05MANILA1614. Accessed January 24, 2012.

National Security Strategy of the United States of America, The. 2002. September. http://merln.ndu.edu/whitepapers/USnss2002.pdf. Accessed May 20, 2012.

National Security Strategy of the United States of America, The. 2006. March. http://www.comw.org/qdr/fulltext/nss2006.pdf. Accessed May 20, 2012.

Nexon, Daniel H. 2011. "Religion and International Relations: No Leap of Faith

Required." In *Religion and International Relations Theory,* edited by Jack Snyder, 141–67. New York: Columbia University Press.

Niksch, Larry. 2007. "Abu-Sayyaf: Target of Philippine-U.S. Anti-Terrorism Cooperation." *Congressional Research Service,* 24 January.

Norfolk, Andrew. 2007. "Hardline Takeover of British Mosques." *Times Online,* 7 September.

Norris, Pippa, and Ronald Inglehart. 2004. *Sacred and Secular: Religion and Politics Worldwide.* Cambridge: Cambridge University Press.

Norton-Taylor, Richard. 2007. "Counter-terrorism Officials Rethink Stance on Muslims." *Guardian,* 20 November.

Nye, Joseph S., Jr. 2002. *The Paradox of American Power.* New York: Oxford University Press.

Nye, Joseph S., Jr. 2005. *Soft Power: The Means to Success in World Politics.* New York: Public Affairs.

Obama, Barack. 2009. "Remarks by the President on a New Beginning." www.whitehouse.gov.

O'Brien, Robert, trans. 2005. *The Stasi Report: The Report of the Committee of Reflection on the Application of the Principle of Secularity in the Republic.* Buffalo, NY: William S. Hein.

OneNews. 2007. "Mosque and Catholic University to Train Imams." 2 October.

Pandith, Farah. 2011. Interview with the author, 16 February.

Peck, James. 2010. *Ideal Illusions: How the U.S. Government Co-Opted Human Rights.* New York: Metropolitan Books.

Pedersen, Lars. 1999. *Newer Islamic Movements in Western Europe.* Aldershot, UK: Ashgate.

Pekala, Mark. 2007. "Muslim Outreach: Senior Advisor Farah Pandith's Meetings in Paris July 25–26." U.S. Embassy, Paris, 14 August. http://www.wikileaks.org/cable/2007/08/07PARIS3402.html. Accessed October 6, 2011.

Peter, Frank. 2003. "Training Imams and the Future of Islam in France." *ISIM Newsletter 13,* December.

Philpott, Daniel. 2002. "The Challenge of September 11 to Secularism in International Relations." *World Politics* 55: 66–95.

"Preventing Extremism Together." 2005. http://www.communities.gov.uk/archived/publications/communities/preventingextremismtogether. Accessed May 20, 2012.

"Preventing Violent Extremism: Winning Hearts and Minds." 2007. UK Department of Communities and Local Government. London: Crown Copyright. http://www.communities.gov.uk/documents/communities/pdf/320752.pdf. Accessed May 20, 2012.

"Preventing Violent Extremism: Next Steps for Communities." 2008. UK Department of Communities and Local Government. London: Crown Copyright. http://www.communities.gov.uk/documents/communities/pdf/896799.pdf. Accessed May 20, 2012.

Prevent Strategy. 2011. The Home Office. www.official-documents.gov.uk.

Quilliam Foundation. www.quilliamfoundation.org.

Ricciardone, Francis J. 2005a. "AFP/DND Talks Produce Progress on Counterterrorism Scenarios." U.S. Embassy, Manila, 10 January. http://www.wikileaks.org/cable/2005/01/05MANILA286.html. Accessed January 24, 2012.

Ricciardone, Francis J. 2005b. "GRP's NSC Gropes For Answers to Islamist Extremism." U.S. Embassy, Manila, 21 April. http://www.wikileaks.org/cable/2005/04/05MANILA1817.html. Accessed January 24, 2012.

Ricciardone, Francis J. 2005c. "Madrasah Teacher Training Project Underway in the Philippines." U.S. Embassy, Manila, 10 January. http://www.wikileaks.org/cable/2005/01/05MANILA106.html. Accessed January 24, 2012.

Ricciardone, Francis J. 2005d. "Further Progress in Counterterrorism Scenario Talks." U.S. Embassy, Manila, 7 March. http://www.wikileaks.org/cable/2005/03/05MANILA1056.html. Accessed January 24, 2012.

Rotar, Igor. 2004. "Imams and Mosque Education under State Control." *Forum 18 News Service,* 15 September. http://www.forum18.org/Archive.php?article_id=411. Accessed September 9, 2010.

Rudolph, Susan Hoeber, and James Piscatori, eds. 1997. *Transnational Religion and Fading States.* Boulder: Westview Press.

Said, Edward W. 1979. *Orientalism.* New York: Vintage Books.

Samers, Michael E. 2003. "Diaspora Unbound: Muslim Identity and the Erratic Regulation of Islam in France." *International Journal of Population Geography* 9:351–64.

Samuel, Henry. 2008. "Nicolas Sarkozy in Row Over Secularism." *Telegraph,* 14 February.

Sarkozy, Nicolas. 2002. "COMOR Meeting: Speech by M. Nicolas Sarkozy, Minister of the Interior, Internal Security and Local Freedoms, Paris." 20 June.

Sarkozy, Nicolas. 2003a. "Visit to Egypt: Interview Given by M. Nicolas Sarkozy to 'France 2.'" 30 December.

Sarkozy, Nicolas. 2003b. "Twentieth Annual Meeting of the Union of France's Islamic Organizations: Speech by M. Nicolas Sarkozy, Le Bourget." 19 April.

Sarkozy, Nicolas. 2005. *La Republique, Les Religions, L'Esperence.* New York: Pocket Books.

Sarkozy, Nicolas 2007a. "Speech at the Opening of the Conference of Ambassadors IV." 27 August.

Sarkozy, Nicolas. 2007b. "Fifteenth Ambassadors Conference Speech." 27 August.

Sarkozy, Nicolas. 2007c. "Franco-Moroccan Business Meeting—Speech by M. Nicolas Sarkozy." 24 October.

Sarkozy, Nicolas. 2007d. "Speech by the President of the Republic at the University of Mentouri-Constantine." 5 December.

Sarkozy, Nicolas. 2007e. "Discours de Nicolas Sarkozy au Palais du Latran." 20 December. http://www.vigile.net/Discours-de-Nicolas-Sarkozy-au. Accessed October 28, 2010.

Sarkozy, Nicolas. 2008a. "Discours de Nicolas Sarkozy devant le Conseil Consultatif Saodien." 14 January. www.voltairenet.org/article 154955.html.

Sarkozy, Nicolas. 2008b. "Speech by M. Nicolas Sarkozy Before the Students of the National Institute of Applied Science and Technology, Tunis." 30 April.

Satloff, Robert. 2000. "U.S. Policy Toward Islamism: A Theoretical and Operational Overview." New York: Council on Foreign Relations.

Scarborough, Rowan. 2010. "Obama at Odds with Petraeus Doctrine on 'Islam.'" *Washington Times,* 11 July.

Schilling, Heinz. 1986. "The Reformation and the Rise of the Early Modern State." In *Luther and the Modern State in Germany,* edited by James D. Tracy, 21–30. Kirksville, MO: Sixteenth Century Journal Publisher.

Schmidt, Pierre. 2007. "L'Institut Catholique de Paris Pourrait Former Des Imams." LaCroix.com. 24 September.

Seiple, Robert, and Dennis Hoover, eds. 2004. *Religion and Security: The New Nexus in International Relations.* New York: Rowman and Littlefield.

Shariati, Ali. 1981. *Man and Islam.* Houston: Free Islamic Literature.

Shepherd, Jessica. 2007. "Imams are not the Solution to Terrorism." *Guardian,* 12 June.

Siemon-Netto, Uwe. 2003. "France Promotes Moderate Islam." *United Press International* ,21 April.

Slack, James. 2009a. "Second Muslim Group Faces Having Links Severed with Government over Extremism Row." *Daily Mail Online,* 25 March. http://www.daily mail.co.uk/news/article-1164891. Accessed May 19, 2012.

Slack, James. 2009b. "Hazel Blears Cuts Ties to Muslim Council of Britain After it Refuses to Condemn Controversial Senior Member." *Daily Mail Online,* 25 March. http://www.dailymail.co.uk/news/article-1164613.

Smith, Brian K. 1989. *Reflections on Resemblance, Ritual, and Religion.* New York: Oxford University Press.

Smith, Jacqui. 2008a. "Countering Terrorism in a Democracy." 3 June. http://press. homeoffice.gov.uk/Speeches/countering-terrorism-democracy.html. Accessed April 15, 2010.

Smith, Jacqui. 2008b. "Speech to the Institute for Public Policy Research." 15 October. http://press.homeoffice.gov.uk/Speeches/speech-to-ippr.html. Accessed April 15, 2010.

Smith, Jacqui. 2008c. "Pursue Prevent Protect Prepare: The United Kingdom's Strategy for Countering International Terrorism." http://merln.ndu.edu/white-papers/UnitedKingdom2009.pdf. Accessed April 15, 2010.

Smith, Jonathan Z. 1998. "Religion, Religions, Religious." In *Critical Terms for Religious Studies,* edited by Mark C. Taylor, 269–84. Chicago: University of Chicago Press.

Snyder, Jack. 2011. "Introduction." In *Religion and International Theory,* edited by Jack Snyder, 1–23. New York: Columbia University Press.

Solomon, Richard H. 2009. "Letter from the President of the United States Institute of Peace." In *Conflict, Identity, and Reform in the Muslim World: Challenges for U.S. Engagement,* edited by Daniel Brumberg and Dina Shehata, ix. Washington, DC: United States Institute of Peace Press.

Spicer, Nick. 2002. "A Search for Islam *a la Francaise.*" *Christian Science Monitor,* 15 July.

Stapleton, Craig. 2005a. "Combating Extremism in France." U.S. Embassy, Paris,

4 October. http://www.wikileaks.org/cable/2005/10/05PARIS6810.html. Accessed October 6, 2011.

Stapleton, Craig. 2005b. "Dialogue with Muslim Moderates and Maghreb Ambassadors on Islam in France." U.S. Embassy, Paris, 6 October. http://www.wikileaks. org/cable/2005/10/05PARIS6890.html. Accessed October 6, 2011.

Stapleton, Craig. 2005c. "French Muslim Council Election Results." U.S. Embassy, Paris, 1 July. http://www.wikileaks.org/cable/2005/07/05PARIS4644. Accessed October 6, 2011.

Stapleton, Craig. 2005d. "Counter-Terrorism Consultations with the French, Part 2 of 2." U.S. Embassy, Paris, 7 July. http://www.wikileaks.org/ cable/2005/07/05PARIS4750.html. Accessed October 6, 2011.

Stapleton, Craig. 2006a. "French Muslim Protests of Mohammed Cartoons Grow in Size, Remain Peaceful." U.S. Embassy, Paris, 13 February. http://www.wikileaks. org/cable/2006/02/06PARIS915.html. Accessed January 19, 2012.

Stapleton, Craig. 2006b. "French Muslim Leader Describes Bleak Outlook for Suburban Youth, Hails U.S. Integration Model." U.S. Embassy, Paris, 7 April. http://www.wikileaks.org/cable/2006/04/06PARIS2314.html. Accessed October 6, 2011.

Stapleton, Craig. 2006c. "French Muslim Leader: Yes to France, But No to Sarkozy's 'Official Islam.'" U.S. Embassy, Paris, 26 September. http://www.wikileaks.org/ cable/2006/09/06PARIS6442.html. Accessed October 6, 2011.

Stern, Jessica. 2010. "Mind over Martyr: How to Deradicalize Islamic Extremists." *Foreign Affairs,* January/February, 95–108.

Stritzel, H. 2007. "Towards a Theory of Securitization: Copenhagen and Beyond." *European Journal of International Relations* 13 (3): 357–83.

Sukma, Rizal, and Clara Joewono, eds. 2007. *Islamic Thought and Movements in Contemporary Indonesia.* Yogyakarta, Indonesia: Center for Strategic and International Studies.

Task Force Bayonet Public Affairs. 2010. "TF Bayonet, TF Nashmi Reach Afghans with First-Ever Program." 3 September.

Thistlewaite, Susan Brooks. 2010. "Religion: The Smartest Power of All." *Washington Post Online,* 22 February. http://onfaith.washingtonpost.com/onfaith/pan elists/susan_brooks_thistlethwaite/2010/02/get_religion_or_go_home.html. Accessed May 19, 2012.

Thomas, Scott. 2005. *The Global Resurgence of Religion and the Transformation of International Relations.* New York: Palgrave.

Thomas, Paul. 2010. "Failed and Friendless: The UK's Preventing Violent Extremism Program." *British Journal of Politics and International Relations* (12): 442–58.

Travis, Alan. 2007. "Struggling Home Office Split up to Combat Terrorism." *Guardian,* 30 March.

Travis, Alan. 2010. "Theresa May Pledges Significant Reform of Counter-Terrorism Laws." *Guardian,* 3 November.

Turner, Bryan S. 2002. "Sovereignty and Emergency: Political Theology, Islam, and American Conservatism." *Theory, Culture & Society* 19 (4): 103–19.

Tuttle, Robert H. 2006. "Tensions Rise Between British Muslims and HMG in the

Wake of Thwarted Terrorist Attack." U.S. Embassy, London, 14 August. http://www.guardian.co.uk/world/us-embassy-cables-documents/74818. Accessed May 19, 2012.

Tuttle, Robert H. 2007a. "EUR Senior Advisor Pandith and S/P Advisor Cohen's Visit to the UK, October 9–14 2007." US Embassy, London, 25 October. http://www.wikileaks.org/cable/2007/10/07LONDON4045.html. Accessed May 19, 2012.

Tuttle, Robert H. 2007b. "DHS Secretary Chertoff's Meeting with Home Secretary Jacqui Smith." US Embassy, London, 21 November. http://wikileaks.org/cable/2007/10/07LONDON4045.html. Accessed May 19, 2012.

UKNSS. 2008. *The National Security Strategy of the United Kingdom: Security in an Interdependent World.* London: Crown Copyright.

United States Army. 2009. *The U.S. Army Stability Operations Field Manual.* Ann Arbor: University of Michigan Press.

U.S. Government Accountability Office. 2006. *U.S. Public Diplomacy: State Department Efforts To Engage Muslim Audiences Lack Certain Communication Elements and Face Significant Challenges.* Washington, DC: United States Government and Accountability Office.

Untermeyer, Chase. 2006. "U/S Hughes Meeting with Qatari Foreign Minister and Sheikha Mozah." U.S. Embassy, Doha, 26 February. http://www.wikileaks.org/cable/2006/02/06DOHA293.html. Accessed January 19, 2012.

Vaughn, Bruce. 2005. "Islam in South and Southeast Asia." 8 February. *Congressional Research Service.*

Vuori, J. 2008. "Illocutionary Logic and Strands of Securitization: Applying the Theory of Securitization to non-Democratic Political Orders." *European Journal of International Relations* 14 (1): 65–99.

Waever, Ole. 1995. "Securitization and Desecuritization." In *On Security,* edited by Ronnie Lipschutz, 46–86. New York: Columbia University Press.

Walt, Stephen. 1991. "The Renaissance of Security Studies." *International Studies Quarterly* 35 (2): 211–39.

Weber, Max. 1963 [1922]. *The Sociology of Religion.* Boston: Beacon Press.

Williams, Michael C. 1998. "Modernity, Identity, and Security: A Comment on the Copenhagen Controversy." *Review of International Studies* 24:435–39.

Williams, Michael C. 2003. "Words, Images, Enemies: Securitization and International Politics." *International Studies Quarterly* 47 (4): 511–31.

Williams, Rhys H. 1996. "Religion as Political Resource: Culture or Ideology?" *Journal for the Scientific Study of Religion* 35 (4): 368–78.

Yahmid, Hadi. 2009. "French Imams Study Secularism." IslamOnline, 22 February.

Yandura, Matthew J. 2011. "Voices of Moderate Islam." *Information Operations Journal* 3, no. 1 (March): 10–28.

York, Byron. 2010. "NASA's New Mission: Building Ties to Muslim World." *San Francisco Examiner,* 6 July.

Index

Printed and bound by CPI Group (UK) Ltd, Croydon, CR0 4YY

10/06/2025